# TWIN FLAMES:
## THE TRUTH & THE JOURNEY

# TWIN FLAMES:
## THE TRUTH & THE JOURNEY

*Nichole X. Clarke, MS*

gatekeeper press™
Tampa, Florida

The views and opinions expressed in this book are solely those of the author and do not necessarily reflect the views or opinions of Gatekeeper Press. Gatekeeper Press is not to be held responsible for and expressly disclaims responsibility of the content herein.

Twin Flames: The Truth & the Journey

Published by Gatekeeper Press
7853 Gunn Hwy, Suite 209
Tampa, FL 33626
www.GatekeeperPress.com

Copyright © 2022 by Nichole X. Clarke, MS
All rights reserved. Neither this book, nor any parts within it may be sold or reproduced in any form or by any electronic or mechanical means, including information storage and retrieval systems, without permission in writing from the author. The only exception is by a reviewer, who may quote short excerpts in a review.

Library of Congress Control Number: 2022945578

ISBN (paperback): 9781662931451
eISBN: 9781662931468

# Contents

*Preface* .................................................................................. vii

**Chapter 1**   The Path Less Traveled ............................... 1

**Chapter 2**   In the Beginning… .................................... 21

**Chapter 3**   Drifting Down a Sea of Feelings .............. 31

**Chapter 4**   When the Pain Outweighs the Pleasure .... 41

**Chapter 5**   H.A.A.R.S.H. ............................................ 54

**Chapter 6**   Spiritual Gifts/Spiritual Warfare .............. 69

**Chapter 7**   Karmics .................................................... 77

**Chapter 8**   False Flames ............................................. 88

**Chapter 9**   Speaking Truth Unapologetically ............ 94

**Chapter 10**  Union ..................................................... 101

# Preface

## Song: This Is the Right Time
## By: Lisa Stansfield

This book is written primarily from my personal experience as a Divine Feminine. The twin flame journey is undisputedly one of the most profound connections created between two souls, both spiritually and energetically, where these divine counterparts vibrate on the same frequency as one another while triggering and mirroring each other as truly one. The term "twin flame" is a reference or label that has been hackneyed by couples and individuals alike who have declared the intensity of a connection they share with another, whether publicly or privately. Despite the amount of information that is currently circulating about this connection, a huge misconception has still been formed in which contemporary couples have referred to themselves as twin flames, only to discover more times than not they aren't, or alternatively they were involved instead with a false twin or catalyst twin. Many karmics (mostly people but they can also represent situations where lessons need to be learned) give the actual twin flame journey, including those labeled as soulmates and life partners, a very jaded misrepresentation of this connection. The bonds formed from the twin flame journey are all very distinctive, yet strangely they have mutual similarities accompanied by relatable experiences within the relationship dynamic. It's no wonder why so many people are misinformed about whether they are really on the twin flame journey. Serious problems can arise when a person becomes influenced by false narratives based on inaccurate information obtained about a particular connection they've misaligned themselves to. It transmits the dangers of labeling a relationship something it may not be, in turn creating anxiety, false hope, and delusions. Occasionally when an individual does this, they operate mostly from their lower self out of pride and ego, causing them to boastfully assume something about their relationship that may be false or created by falsehoods. Several people view this cosmic love from a rather superficial outlook, codifying extremely warped perceptions of what they believe "true love" means on this journey. For others, like myself, who genuinely are on this expedition, believe me when I tell you at times the phrase "a gift and a curse" seems like an understatement when describing this twin flame experience.

Where do I start? Perhaps I should begin with the most obvious truth. This cosmic connection is indescribable, undeniable, and plainly said, just downright unorthodox to sometimes comprehend. I dare you to attempt to convey to others not on this journey, those to whom you do confess this intergalactic love, the ins and outs of this voyage. More than half of them, if not all of them, will likely presume you are completely insane and immediately begin to judge the sanity of your reality . . . God bless the few in number who do support you, that give you an ear to vent to, and a shoulder to lean and cry on when this tsunami called the "Twin Flame Journey" starts unfolding its massive towers and tidal waves.

To be chosen as a twin flame is an absolute honor. So it doesn't surprise me in the least why so many people claim to be a participant of such an experience or relationship without ever explaining just how difficult and tumultuous the path truly is. I believe with all my heart and soul humanity lives under the illusion of what I like to refer to as the "microwave era," where everything is expected to be done instantaneously, yet sufficiently, all the while avoiding the crucial steps often necessary in order to obtain the desired results anticipated. Plainly put, the work! People these days want what they want when they want it, seldom understanding that in life, some things require time and patience to manifest. Like bread that rises, time is necessary in all areas of life, in addition to love and growth, in order to achieve the desired result one seeks. We all know the microwave is great for heating things up, not exclusively for cooking. It would appear in some instances related to love specifically, people no longer want to make their meals from scratch, nor are they concerned about the preparation required for cooking the meal. All they seem worried about is when they can enjoy the meal. These are the same individuals who believe concocting a meal from scratch requires just too much time, hence the term "soul food." We all know just how much of a rush humanity is in, so people ultimately just settle for fast food, TV dinners, or eating out, which economically is not an option everyone can continuously commit to every day. And quite frankly, even if you could, why would you? It isn't healthy. Are you still with me? I hope I didn't lose you, as I also hope that you do realize I was speaking literally, metaphorically, and figuratively . . . gotta stay with me because if you hadn't realized it yet, I was also referring to the steps and recipe on the manifestation of love.

A major misconception about the connection is the self-proclaimed entitlement of the label "twin flame" many people give themselves before really understanding whether or not this reference applies to them or their current relationship situation. Twins who exist in the present timeline did not consciously choose this journey in the 3D initially. Yes, both counterparts agreed to this journey before they were born. However, I do not personally know of any twins who have testified to learning about the twin flame journey one day, then suddenly started referring to themselves as a twin flame the next day. I, like many divine counterparts, was well on my journey prior to discovering what the journey was. Obviously, every twin flame experience differs from person to person. However, I personally have yet to meet any authentic twins on the journey who discovered they were twins only after already being in a committed relationship for several years. It counteracts and is quite counterproductive to the stages of this journey. And let me tell you, if you weren't aware: there are levels to this journey. The separation stage is a major component experienced on the journey that all twins experience . . . but I'll get into that a little later. As mentioned, there are stages the twins, regardless of how and when the stages appear in their lives, independently must encounter and successfully complete. Twins did not consciously ask for this path like so many do now since this journey has become so popular and widely recognized. The journey and path were already chosen for them. I can confidently assure you if you ask any true Divine Masculine or Divine Feminine about the truth regarding this connection, you will most certainly receive a different narrative than the one you may have heard or witnessed through mainstream media.

The love manifested between the Divine Masculine and the Divine Feminine is a voyage through uncharted waters that very few in this lifetime have sailed . . . yet worth every single wave crashed along the shores. Love grounded in truth, love that is unconditional, and love that is patient is what centers the twin flame journey. The exact love mentioned in 1 Corinthians 13:4–7 in the Holy Bible. The love we often witness broadcasted in the world or hear about in the songs we listen to, on more occasions than a few, generally is manipulated, staged, and controlled to project "love" in a particular way. It is a love that sometimes favors many of the toxicities or toxic behaviors we display with others, projecting these toxicities as some weird hidden clause that's attached to love. Please check the fine print people. That isn't love. Whether you understand it or not, marriage is a contract, but love is the fine print. Believe it or not, everyone married isn't in love. Take that as it resonates. People have inadvertently shamelessly exchanged unconditional love for toxic unhealthy love and/or superficial gratifications, while enabling karmic connections in their lives that become repetitive. The results for most of these individuals end with them failing to learn the lesson in the karmic cycle they were bound to in the first place, thus enabling the cycle to repeat itself with the same plot, just different characters. (Karmic Wheel)

The twin flame journey is anything but a walk in the park. My overall experience has been both enlightening and exhausting. However, I am a warrior and I'm most certainly on the battlefield for my Lord! As the hymn so eloquently goes, "And I promised him that I, would serve him till I die, yes I'm on the battlefield for my Lord." While in the eye of the downpour, it becomes difficult, and for many, almost impossible to appreciate the rain when weathering the storm. This journey has supplied me with an appreciation for the storms in my life. It is only then one can observe their seeds that were once planted in the dirt begin to flourish and grow. I thank God every day for choosing me as a Divine Feminine. No one ever said the road would be smooth, but I thank the Lord for cushioning the bumps as he accompanied me the entire way.

## Chapter 1

# The Path Less Traveled

## Song: Love Is Stronger Than Pride
## By: Sade

Well, the time has finally arrived for me to not just tell the tale of the twin flame journey, but to also speak the truth about my own twin flame experience. My reasons for writing this book are governed in the authenticity of who I am and my experience on the journey. As a Divine Feminine, healer, and lightworker, it is my duty to speak the truth that might expose the falsehoods in conjunction with this rare and intense connection. One of my missions is to assist the collectives (Divine Masculine, Divine Feminine, Emperors, Empresses, Starseeds, Indigo/ Rainbow children, etc.) who are also on the path of enlightenment—those searching for guidance and answers. The journey and all it entails allowed me to be reacquainted with my higher self while understanding what my life purpose is. While on this voyage, many things were revealed to me about my true self that I might not have known, let alone been able to heal from had

I never embarked on this journey. In addition to learning more about myself, I was able to better understand the people I interacted with, as well as their true motives and intentions, including those of my divine counterpart.

Often, we as people presume that wherever we are in life and whatever it is we are doing is all we're supposed to be doing. If I were to say I blame the matrix for that misconception, you would just let that go over your head. So I'll just say, I blame this on our inability as humans to embrace evolution and change. Change is inevitable, yet not everyone is receptive to it. Especially people who are stuck in their ways and the familiarity of what they know. Change sometimes can be frightening. It requires learning regenerated tasks while sometimes performing renewed concepts. Unfortunately, people can become rigid and reluctant to anything that differs from what they already know, or a pattern and routine they have already established. We have probably all heard the expression, "Can't teach an old dog new tricks." This would most certainly befit the situation described.

Additionally, my reasons for writing this book have a lot more to do with addressing the lies, misconceptions, and continuous misinformation that constantly is associated with the twin flame journey that more people have gravitated toward than the actual truth behind this rare connection. It would appear there are people in committed relationships, whether healthy or toxic, who have been exposed to the "twin flame" narrative and, without fully educating themselves on the journey, have adopted the term, then applied it to their relationship status before understanding whether the term is even applicable to them. True divine counterparts know firsthand, because they did the work, how frustrating it is to witness false testimonies about this connection when you are on this journey yourself. Honestly, it's rather disrespectful if you ask me. I've noticed that many people who are becoming vocal and transparent about the twin flame journey do so from a very limited perspective. These individuals usually tend to focus on a one-dimensional view of the voyage, which in most cases would be the unconditional love demonstrated and shared amongst the counterparts. However, the actual journey entails far more depth and requires much more understanding.

Recently, the term "twin flame" found its way to Hollywood, although I honestly have a burdensome time trusting the validity of some of these "celebrity twin flames." My reasons for this stem from the mere fact that people in Hollywood alleging to be twins seem to focus primarily only on public displays of affection and confessions of love when they reveal to the world that they are twins, as opposed to discussing the additional variables and essential factors also outlined within the course of the journey. Yes, love is certainly a primary factor involved. However, I have yet to hear anything else spoken in relation to the twin flame journey other than the obvious "love" uttered from these "celebrity twins." There are so many more components involved that people alleging to be twins aren't mentioning or discussing, which is a disservice to the collectives at large. Several people have heard the expression "twin flame." However, while researching multitudes of information about the connection, people have discovered there exists data that sometimes contradicts other information researched, which is why in my heart opinion, the best information is often based on experience and not always book knowledge. Individuals, specifically those who aren't experiencing this connection, can easily be led astray based on false perceptions and inaccurate misinformation.

So, what is this twin flame journey all about then? If you research the term, you will discover that the purpose of a twin flame relationship is to awaken you to your untapped potential and ignite a fire deep inside of you. According to Savvas, "This relationship pushes you to do and be better." In other words, it propels you forward to become the best version of yourself. Contrary to popular belief, the journey isn't predominately focused on the union of the Divine Masculine and Divine Feminine. Its focal point is elevating to one's higher self while establishing a relationship with the Divine or the creator of your divinity, all the while learning to love the self in order to love another unconditionally. There are so many other lessons and stages experienced throughout this journey that need be addressed, like the notorious shadow work you might have previously heard mentioned from many readers, motivational speakers, and spiritualists, accompanied by the dark night of the soul that occurs with all twins, although not necessarily at the same time or in the exact same manner. However, many stages of the twin flame journey simply are unavoidable. It comes with the journey and the healing acquired within the journey.

The twin flame journey in no form or fashion declares this relationship to be better than a soulmate relationship or any other bond formed between two people built on love. It's this very misconception that has so many people thinking they're on this journey when they truthfully aren't. They think saying they are a "twin" validates the authenticity of their relationship as true love. On the contrary, most twins truly on this voyage operate completely opposite to those vocally declaring they are on the journey. Why is that you ask? One reason has a great deal to do with the actual truth about this journey verses the misappropriated tales that get ushered to the masses. The work that goes into this connection is far from tranquil. The turbulence of emotions, the stages of the runner/chaser phases, the separation period, the dark night of the soul, the shadow work, the healing, the building of boundaries, and the unresolved childhood traumas experienced are all elements aligned with this journey that get overshadowed. Perhaps due to the latest influx of the discovery of the twin flame journey, people and their overwhelming obsession to constantly feel a need to compete with one another usually are the same ones who tend to automatically assume they are a twin because it sounds alluring and exclusive. Seriously, I mean, who wouldn't want a connection based on unconditional love that is blessed from the highest God? However, it's like the saying goes: "They want the baby, but they don't want the labor pains that come along with the baby." That's typical for the caliber of humans we have become. Instant gratification like I mentioned earlier regarding the microwave era is the mentality of many people in the 21st century. We live in an extremely egotistical society fueled by clout chasing and attention seekers who are obsessed with superficialities and popularity. Once the twin flame journey started trending, it was no surprise to me at all the influx of people who were announcing they were twins. But the question for me became, how many truly are versus how many are just hitching a ride on the bandwagon?

Why does it matter? Oh, when it comes to me, it matters a great deal because this twin flame journey has completely transformed my entire life and was anything but lollipops and gumdrops, as it is often seen. It realigned me to step into my full power in recognizing who I am and not who people said I was. The falsehoods and misinformation clearly are frustrating to witness when you are a Divine Feminine who did the work on this journey. Especially when the journey is being mentioned by others, where you seldom ever hear about the test, trials, and tribulations of the union and the extensive work and healing that goes into this connection. The journey is so much more than playing the part. It is beyond a physical connection; it is a spiritual bond. The depth of the connection involved in this journey is grounded in love with God the Divine, with the self, and with your counterpart is far more life-altering and influential than believing that this journey is strictly about a love shared unconditionally between partners. That's only a portion of this bond.

It makes a significant difference to me what information is being delivered to the collectives regarding this journey because I am a lightworker serving humanity and the collectives who are on this journey searching for answers, guidance, and their soul families. What some people don't want to accept as the truth is that not everyone has a twin flame, nor will everyone experience this connection. There are many tarot readers, spiritualists, and other practitioners who are unfortunately confusing collectives with false narratives such as that mentioned and so much more, in which untruths about this connection are developing more rapidly than the actual awareness about this divinely ordained relationship.

The majority of the people I've encountered in the world do not like to feel excluded (unhealed people mostly) from things. They have severe trauma with abandonment issues. These suppressed emotions of unresolved abandonment issues, as well as unhealed childhood trauma and abuse that may have lain dormant from their past, begin to surface. The feeling of "exclusion" operates as a trigger, thus allowing an individual to react defensively, often in a toxic or impulsive response toward a person, place, thing, or situation where it's perceived the individual is being prohibited from gaining access, alignment, or involvement to something that someone else is.

Truthfully spoken, the twin flame journey is an extremely rare connection and not nearly as common as the masses assume it to be. This journey is not designed for everyone in this world simply because everyone in this world can't endure the aftermath of what comes along with the connection. The tolerance level, strength, discipline, and faith we have as inherent human beings differ from person to person, which is why everyone realistically will not have this experience. However, just to know it truly exists is rewarding even if you yourself are not a twin flame. I must admit, as a Divine Feminine, frequently I would find myself becoming frustrated with the narrative projected to the world about the twin flame journey and how over-romanticized the journey is portrayed as. Ask any true Divine Masculine and Divine Feminine about this connection and they will tell you, this journey is WORK, WORK, and just when you thought you were done, MORE WORK. Surprisingly, this is what I don't hear discussed about this journey, and I'm baffled by the very audacity, because the WORK demonstrated in the connection is one of the key elements of the twin flame journey. In order to get to "happily ever after," the work must be initiated and completed.

The work primarily is done first on the self. As you successfully elevate to higher levels of authenticity of the self, and when you have successfully completed the necessary stages of intense shadow work for growth and healing, it then allows karmic cycles (lessons that are often repeated in lifetimes due to a failure to accept the truth or make the right choices) to complete and close out. Even though all twin flames have a very uniquely individualized encounter of the journey that certainly differs for each person, there are, however, shared elements of some of these stages within this journey that ALL twins embark on along the way.

So, guys, this is where my passion to write this book fits into the equation. I've been divinely guided to discuss the truth about this journey from the perception of someone who is on the journey, and not from a blogger analysis nor a hypothetical or theoretical perspective. Was I nervous to write this book, at first? Yes, I was battling with my ego about whether I should even go forward with it in fear of harsh criticism and ridicule from people until the Holy Spirit reminded me why it needed to be done, and why I needed to be the one to do it! It's much bigger than me, as is the journey, because it's way bigger than just a love story. It's a cosmic shift toward a better world in which we are to love God and love one another equally, treating one another with respect and common decency. instead of warring, killing, and competing with one another, we need to show appreciation to Mother Gaia by respecting our natural resources given to us freely that we so carelessly take for granted.

I can certainly resonate with how lonely a person might feel in the initial stages of this journey. The stages where you don't even know you're on a twin flame journey. All you seem to know is something about this connection you share with another person is one of a kind. Those reading this book who are true twins on this path know when you seek answers, you will find them. I have been blessed to have some amazing guides assist me on my journey. If you read this book and remember nothing at all, know that the twin flame journey is a divinely ordained connection from God. It's more sophisticated than simply just loving someone. This is a soul contract. If you believe yourself to be on this journey yet lack a personal relationship with God/ Divine/Source and he is not the main attraction in your connection, sorry to be the bearer of bad news while bursting your bubble, but you aren't on the twin flame journey.

As human beings, we are guilty of perceiving things in life according to how we choose/wish to see things and rarely for what things truly are. When essential components to this journey aren't mentioned or discussed, I, as an Empress, am left with no choice but to doubt the truth in people's allegations of being a twin flame, and to provide clarity about this sacred bond. People projecting one-sided perceptions of this journey leave me to question the authenticity behind the claims of these individuals alleging to be on the voyage.

I am extremely grateful for the journey in more ways than one. I would like to take a moment to thank some very important people in my life who, whether directly or indirectly, influenced me to write the book. First and foremost, I want to give honor to God the Father, Jesus Christ the Son, and the Holy Spirit the comforter, who I humbly and gratefully thank every day for choosing me to be a Divine Feminine. If it were not for God, Lord knows where I would have been in life. Thank you, Lord, for showing me the truth throughout this entire journey and for the everlasting protection you've granted my family and me while I have been on the battlefield of this spiritual warfare. Like the beautiful title of the Marvin Sapp song, "I never would have made it without you," Lord. Your promises are eternal, and I am forever grateful for you never leaving my side. I can honestly never thank you enough, but I promise I'll try anyway.

To my beautiful princesses Heavenly Treasure and Adoringly Grace, I want you to know that I wrote this book in truth, love, compassion, and reverence for the journey and for others like me who have also embarked on this expedition into Wonderland. It's possible I might be judged harshly, critically, and severely, but if that should be so, know that I will be fine because I did what the Lord asked of me: to speak my truth. No matter what, girls, never be silenced nor afraid to speak "Your Truth"! Regardless of what this insensitive world will attempt to throw your direction, God our Father, who art in heaven, hallowed be thy name, will always vindicate the truth because we serve a God of justice. Heavenly, special thanks for your relentless ability to understand my pain even when words were often never spoken about what I was battling. As I made radical transformations to become the woman I am today, there you were pushing me to keep moving forward. For the last two years, you have been a pillar of strength and support for me. You encouraged me continuously to do something in life we are often advised not to do, which is follow my heart. You never once judged me. Instead, you were always there to console and comfort me on those occasions when I just didn't have the power in me to progress forward. You did all this accompanied by hugs, love, and plenty of tissue for every tear I shed. I love you immensely!

Thank you, Dad (Jazzy Jodie), for always allowing me to be my authentic self, even before I had an overall understanding of who I am. Love conquers all indeed! I sincerely appreciate you and thank you for respecting my decisions and choices to live life according to my truth and not the opinions of others, and to be who I am while I do what it is I do. Thank you, Mom (Yvette) and Pop (Benji), for the understanding while I was in the initial stages of the journey. I know how difficult it may have been at times in the beginning, watching me deal with an experience unfamiliar to you both. As you were able to witness firsthand, the journey revamped and metamorphosed me into a butterfly while altering me to become a more evolved version of myself. I want to give gratitude and appreciation for remaining open-minded to the process I was becoming a part of. Mom, we didn't always see eye to eye on this journey, especially the times when you were operating out of fear of the unknown. However, no matter whether you believed me or didn't, I thank you for trusting in God to know I was being guided and led by none other than the Holy Spirit. Anytime you can get me to change, it must be the hand of God involved. Thank you for respecting my decisions to make my own choices and to lead my own life.

To my older sister Vena, thank you for not telling the family I had finally lost it and had people commit my black ass to a hospital somewhere, lol, for some form of mental disturbance and psychological breakdown. Lord knows how judgmental the inhabitants of this world are. You've been my sister for thirty-nine years, and you of all people know I couldn't care less how people see me, how they feel toward me, or what their opinions are about me. My priority will always be what I think and feel about myself. Simply said, thanks for not making fun of me. This time it wasn't the weed, lol. Thank you, Krystal, for all your loyalty and support. You are and always have been a solid companion who is considered family to me. Thank you for being a shoulder I could cry on and an ear to vent to. I love you. To my brother, Nathaniel, to say I love you does no justice or equivalency for the admiration I have for you. Loyalty should be your name! I have always been grateful for your companionship, profound knowledge, and understanding, but above all this, your relentless support and devotion. Bro, I got you! Special acknowledgment to Phyllis, Dana, Izzy, and Maria. Thanks for the role you play in my life.

There are so many others I want to say thank you to, and if I didn't mention your name, it doesn't mean I think any less of you. From my heart to yours, those who know, know, and I sincerely thank you. Too many names to address but know that I love you and appreciate you all the same. You know who you are. To the pastors, ministers, tarot readers, intuitive readers, mediums, clairvoyants, spiritual advisors, and psychics, I sincerely appreciate you all more than my words could elaborate. Thank you for the prayers, love sent, and messages received. Special thanks to Pastor/Dr. J. Albert Bush from Walker Memorial Church in the Bronx for his sermons, prayers, teachings, guidance, and love. The commonality lies in the love for God shared. May God continue to bless him and everyone who has helped guide me on my path. Special recognition goes out to some amazing readers who, in one way or another, assisted me on my twin flame journey. Thank you to Vinetta Kumar from Twin Flame Union, Beti Kotevski from Twin Light Tarot, Divine Clarity47, Daniella from Goddess Energy, Frankie from Frankie's Just Tarot, Satija from Satija Tarot, Spiritual Sag, the Dream Clairvoyant, Sun Moon And Stars Intuitive, Harriet from Light House Tarot, Jennifer from Soul Source Tarot, Unique Tarot LLC, Empress Bella, also known as Intuitivegoddess333, The Ghetto Nun (Am I Trippin or Naw Tarot), Daisy (Professional High Priestess), Sent Starr 555, Queen of Light, Prosper Goddess Pey Tarot, Tiff's Tarot, Chanel Bader Tarot and Guidance, Virgo the Oracle Modern Mystic, the Lotus Goddess-Divine Love, Heaven Sent, Baba Jolie Guided Messages, Ali's Tarot, All Eternal Love Tarot Twin Flame Specialist, Spiritual Beauty, Cognitive Tvsia, Mystic Beauutie LLC, Monica from the Love Messages Inc, Kimberkiss Cosmic Tarot, the Serendipity Tarot LLC, Crowned Queen Tarot, Exclusively Intuitive, Ignatuis Wallace Tree of Life Messages, High Priestess

Intuition, JDS Tarot, Rich Lopp, the Leo King, Raising from the Ashes Tarot, Kyra's Krystal Vision's, 222 Tarot, Love Pearl Hawkins, Starseed Goddess Hathor 777, Queen of Wands, Water Star Vibes, Catherine Atkins, Your Inner Chakras LLC, Intuitive Envisions 1111, Patrizia 1111, the Divine Storm 369, Butch Tarot, Sister Moon Tarot, Guided by Angels, Soulful Revolution, LizzyLeeThaGreat DivineStarSeedGoddess, Mami Wata Tarot, HeavenSent, Turning Tides Tarot, Light Channelings, Astraea 5d, Hidden Gems Tarot, Cloud Whispers McQueen Tarot, TaylorRae 777, 222 Tarot, Twin D and Psychic Investigations Tarot.

At some point in my quest every one of these amazing readers, lightworkers, and spiritual advisors has made a positive impact on my journey. I genuinely love every one of them! I am thankful for the truth, honesty, and clarity I've received in their messages guided from the Spirit to the collectives. I know I speak for the collectives at large when I say to all the amazing tarot readers, thanks for the love and compassion you have for humanity to do what you do despite what negative projections come your way about who you are and what you do. Thank you for your service while raising the vibrations on the planet. And so, it begins.

Let me first begin by stating that the details you are reading about the twin flame journey are predominately from my experience and not just information solely derived from books, research, or Google searches. I am discussing things I know about this journey based on my involvement with this connection. It's not unlikely to hear particulars about the twin flame journey from individuals who aren't twins, nor am I suggesting that because you are not a twin flame you can't be familiarized and knowledgeable about the subject. However, in my absolute opinion, I believe no one knows this journey better than an individual who's on the journey. Those of you who are reading this book who are unfamiliar with the storyline, please allow me to enlighten you.

This journey is unlike any connection experienced between two people. Research on the history of the connection states that twins share the same soul that was originally one, but it was split into two in a past lifetime and is now divided and shared amongst each of the counterparts. Let's begin first with some common misconceptions about twin flames. Here are some questions often asked in relation to the journey and the twins that I've come across on several occasions throughout my journey.

1. Is it possible to have more than one twin flame?

    No. In your lifetime you can have several encounters with many soulmates, including karmic soulmates as well, but if you are one of the few rare souls chosen on this journey, you have only one twin flame.

2. Can your family members or a close friend be your twin flame?

    No. Certainly it's possible to establish soul contracts and connections with family members and friends as soulmates, but not as a twin flame. This applies to children and animals also. According to AHNGREATLIFE, a twin flame is someone who catapults your spiritual awakening. A soulmate is someone who can be platonically or romantically connected to your soul throughout lifetimes as a companion. Soulmates can help you grow, prosper, and heal in life in many positive ways. A karmic is an ill-fated soul connection that is meant to mirror your darkest energies and redirect your soul trajectory toward your highest good, but not before destroying a part of you.

3. Does everyone have a twin flame?

No. Unfortunately, the truthful response to this question is not a favorable reply for everyone. I have discovered many websites and readers in the past proclaiming the twin flame journey as if every person in the world will encounter this experience at some stage in their lives. However, this is false and quite misleading. Any true Divine Masculine/ Divine Feminine or true spiritualist will confirm that the TF journey is an extremely intense, strange, and rare life experience operated on a never-ending roller coaster of hidden emotions and suppressed negative thought patterns as you learn to rebuild and love yourself. This requires replacing fear with faith. The truth is, we as people are not alike, nor are we created to withstand the same trials, tribulations, and lessons. This plays a critical role in why everyone will not have this encounter. Far too many people have been misled or they themselves have assisted in misleading the collectives with a lot of lies and, plainly said, a bunch of inaccurate information that results in the production of a massive overload of confusion and perplexity regarding this divine union. Plainly said, a whole bunch of bullshit.

Confusion, if you didn't know, is not in alignment with God. The devil manifests in confusion, doubt, and fear. Spiritual warfare attacks your mental stability, causing you to be hesitant toward your inner intuition as you display uncertainty about the decisions and choices you know you are being guided to make. What many people fail to acknowledge in this connection is that the journey itself is ordained by God. I believe that Jesus is the truth, and he always brings clarity. I understand many will read this book who do not believe in the same spiritual practices as me, and that is perfectly fine. Whether you practice Christianity, Kemetic Orthodoxy, Islam, Judaism, Buddhism, Hinduism, or any other form of religion or divinity, to be on this journey, one must first have a personal relationship with their source of creation. If the God of your understanding is excluded from the journey, then I promise you, you are not on the journey you think you are on. Whenever I notice this, it becomes conformation to me just how commercialized the truth about this journey has become. People have truly helped orchestrate this sacred union as a passing trend and fad.

As an empath I naturally can understand how easily people can become confused and misguided into placing labels on their relationships due to social pressure, popularity, and ego, but the twin flame journey, when discussed, should always be discussed in truth and honesty. There is no room for the ego in this connection, hence why both divine counterparts experience what is known as the dark night of the soul, which is nothing more than an intensified ego death. For goodness' sake, guys, this is a divine relationship, not to be mistaken or seen as another notch on a person's ego-centered belt to prove some overzealous cosmic bond that exists, but in reality doesn't because it wasn't a twin flame connection to begin with. Let's not forget that I already explained earlier that this relationship requires WORK, WORK, and more WORK. Work on yourself, on your connection to God, and work toward the unconditional love you have for your divine counterpart. Yes, this relationship shared amongst lovers is the highest vibration of love encountered. However, this journey is about much more than just saying you're a twin flame and being all lovey-dovey. The real question is, do you understand the journey you believe you're on? Are you sure without a doubt the love of your life is your twin flame, or is your ego just telling you that it is?

Regardless of how you encounter your unique experiences on the journey, all twins go through similar stages because it's divinely guided to operate that way. It's all part of the process. Hence, the phrase often heard, "Trust the process." If you are involved in a committed relationship and believe it to be a twin flame, yet you only speak about love exclusively while failing to bridge a connection to a higher source in the dynamic of your bond, it doesn't mean your relationship isn't wonderful and amazing. It just means it's not a twin flame relationship and that is completely fine. The overall distinction between the twin flame journey and any other intimate relationship deals primarily with a spiritual interrelatedness that does not operate on the same guidelines as 3D matrix relationships. These are your common relationships where love is portrayed and symbolized in superficial and materialistic ways based on shallow external factors involving aesthetic looks, wealth, status, power, and influence.

# Chapter 2

# In the Beginning...

## Song: After the Pain

## By: Betty Wright

When I tell you this journey hit me like a wrecking ball, I kid you not. I'm in no way whatsoever exaggerating the statement by any means. Those of you who know from your own experience, you know. However, for those who don't, listen up . . . The twin flame journey literally came into my life out of nowhere. I never saw it coming, nor did I envision such a situation ever occurring. This is the type of shit movies are made from. To this day, I sometimes find myself saying out loud to my spirit guides, "I was just minding my own business. I didn't ask for this." This great awakening/journey required me to heal many bruises and scars along the way, mostly wounds that I didn't even know were there or still existed. It was after the pain that I smiled, thinking back to the moments when I felt pain the most.

So, it was 2019, August to be exact, when my life as I knew it changed and there was no going back to what life was before 08/19/19. I honestly must say 2019 was an awesome year for me. It was the year I finally started going places and doing things I liked to do. That might sound cheesy to some of you guys, but the truth is my life didn't allow me to travel, go out every weekend, or things of that sort. Regardless, I still appreciated everything I had and have worked very hard to procure the things I've obtained in life. I am a single mom, so there was never time or extra funds for me to travel and go many places. There are many reasons for that, all of which were beyond my control. I kid you not, I literally just got on a plane for the first time in my life in April 2021. No lie. And as I write this book, I haven't been on another flight since.

It's no secret I am a huge hip-hop junkie and music fanatic. I love music and always will, so much so I tattooed it on my chest . . . literally! Music hits different for me than it may for others. For some, it's simply good sounds, good lyrics, and a good beat. For me, it's the emotions, messages, truth, inspiration, and love behind the good sound, good lyrics, and good beat that does is for me. My favorite rapper of all time is none other than Jay-Z, so when I learned he was coming to Webster Hall, I made it my business to be there. A lot of people criticized the amount of money I paid to see him, and I laughed because the way I saw it, for starters, they didn't pay—I did. Happily. So fuck was they so bothered by? Secondly, I wasn't complaining. And thirdly, the moment was priceless and that's what I as a fan

## In the Beginning...

paid for. Like I said earlier, music hits differently for me. That event was epic by the way. I left the concert when it was over feeling so euphoric. Idk, it could've been the cups of Jack and Coke I was tossing back or the moment for me all together, but I vowed when I reached my apartment, life for me was going to be different. The frequency that was transmuting that night was life-changing.

Something about 2019 had me at concert event after event. Sometime during the month of June, I went to the Masters of Ceremony concert at the Barclays and saw DMX (R.I.P.), the Lox, Snoop, Camron, and others and had the time of my life. Later in September, I went back to the Barclays to see Blink 182 and Lil Wayne and had a blast. I was content with life; I mean I was going through some things, but shit, who wasn't? I've lived my life trying not to complain too often, if at all, knowing that somewhere, someplace, another person is wishing to have the things I'm complaining about. The path I've traveled certainly hasn't been the easiest, but my perseverance is incredible. I knew very well that the odds were stacked against me, but that never once made me feel inferior or incapable of pursuing my goals and aspirations. I was going to get it done by any means necessary. Thanks, Malcolm, by the way!

At the time, I was 36 years old, a former ward of state who no one probably thought would have accomplished all I had. A single mom of two beautiful daughters who worked as a paralegal for a Bronx public defender's office for five years. Not too shabby if I say so myself. I obtained my master's degree from Monroe College in Criminal Justice with a specialization in Human Service, where to this day, I'm reminded of my experience of higher learning by the memories of my student loans. Nonetheless, although I was extremely proud of myself and my personal academic achievements, I would periodically have these moments where I felt a void within me. Like a desire or calling that had yet to be fulfilled. I couldn't quite make out what it was, but my soul was craving an attainment that I had never known.

I wasn't really dating and wasn't in a rush. No matter who I met, they just weren't "Him." I did not know who "Him" was at the time, but I knew a feeling would let me know for sure. I've never been the kind of woman who pursued a dude based on superficialities like money. However, that didn't mean I was going to settle for a bum either. And just so we are clear, a bum by my definition also refers to a stagnant mindset just as much as it is often used to refer to homeless, disenfranchised people. One of my main reasons for not worrying about another man's money was I was far too consumed with focusing on my own. If I know nothing at all, I've known how to be self-sufficient and independent since the age of seventeen. That's just how long I have been working. Money didn't entice me to deal with a person. My philosophy then was, and always will be, "What is theirs isn't mine, so why would I ever concentrate on what doesn't belong to me?"

Two days before my thirty-seventh birthday my life as I knew it was altered in the most radical and unexpected

## In the Beginning...

way imaginable. That was the day the universe introduced me to my Divine Masculine. I'm not sure exactly what it was about him or that exact moment in time that assured me this situation was unlike any encounter I would ever experience in life, but I was strangely magnetically pulled in his direction and gave little to no resistance whatsoever. Oddly enough, the energy between me and my DM was nostalgic to say the least. We were so compatible that it was scary. It just flowed so effortlessly. Our conversations intertwined so naturally, like spring water racing carelessly through a stream. It just felt right.

What can I say but my truth! I truly tried to operate from a head-over-heart perspective versus the wearing-my-heart-on-my-sleeve outlook, but it was impossible to do. For the next four weeks, I was in an energy field of pure bliss. Funny thing, though. You can't tell me God doesn't have a sense of humor. I kid you not, I personally feel as though he gets a laugh every time someone utters the phrase, "I will never." So, yeah. Hi, how are thou? Allow me to reintroduce myself, because my name is most definitely "I will never." I've learned in life to be mindful of using that phrase. To me, this statement when said turns out to be a damn setup. During many occasions in my life when I stated, "I will never," no matter how long it took, I ended up somehow doing the very thing I stated I would never do. Talk about the irony, right? I realized the last thing you want to do is tell God/the Universe what you are never going to do because, mark my words, you will at some point in your life find yourself digesting those very same words of defiance if you declare you won't do something that God wills for you to do.

In the past, I used to criticize couples in long-distance relationships and often wondered how a long-distance relationship could possibly work. From my perception back then, if there was a lack of / or limited physical interaction, there was no way it would last. To me, there just wasn't any potential for true love in a long-distance relationship. I bet I am not the only person who thought like that or perhaps still does, but this journey showed me just how wrong I was. Some lessons require learning and experience to fully understand. For those of you who have ever experienced having a long-distance relationship and succeeded in making it work, I have all the respect in the world for your bond and discipline. It was during a long-distance encounter I truly understood love, in which time, space, and distance have no effect if in fact it's true love. Again, lessons to learn. Of course, God didn't make this journey easy, which is why everyone isn't on it.

So, there I was, in this bizarre situationship where I couldn't recall ever feeling so emotionally content. I was glowing from the inside out and was forever grateful for the feeling. I guess you can say I wore the feeling on me like clothes, because everyone who I was around noticed the light in me as well. Something about me was just different. And it showed all over my face. To me, it was as though the missing piece of the puzzle, which I hadn't noticed was lost, was found. Suddenly, without any fair warning whatsoever, the intensity of the connection

## In the Beginning...

magnetized so rapidly that I began to envision my DM as the "One." There lay this unexplainable pull toward a man I barely knew but knew better than I knew myself. At first, of course, I was enamored by these waves of emotions. That is, until the universe began to show me confirmations and synchronicities to substantiate our meeting, assuring us both that this engagement between us was by no means coincidental. As a twin flame there are various ways in which the universe will communicate with you. For me, the universe's most consistent way to get my attention, then and now, is demonstrated through signs of synchronicity in numbers. In the very beginning, the synchronicities in numbers were so obvious. I would see my DM's birthday everywhere, as I am sure he would often see mine. I laugh now, because it was only two months ago to this day I noticed for the first time ever in the seven years working where I work that my employee identification number is his birthday. Lol, man, I can't make this shit up.

When I noticed other repetitive numbers that were becoming recurrent, I was guided to investigate more into the numbers I kept seeing and their significance. At the time, the most recurrent numbers I kept noticing were 555. Everywhere I went, there were those numbers— whether it happened to be the time of the day, the numbers on a license plate or a receipt, or a bus/train number—they were everywhere I was. I later discovered 555 speaks all about change. The change could be positive, or it could be negative. But one thing is for sure and two things are for certain, change is influencing your life when you repetitiously continue to see these numbers. And boy did my life change . . .

It didn't stop there. Afterward, I began to also notice the numbers 111, 1111, 222, 333, 888, etc. I discovered all these numbers were in direct alignment with my journey. The number 1111 is a known twin flame number that embodies the frequency of unconditional love, new beginnings, forward movement, achieving success, the completion of a union, and the embracement of your unique individual self. As I continued gaining enlightenment about the correlation of these numbers and this journey, I also came across more useful information that gave clarity to the experience I was having. Due to the nature of my job and my life and the nature of my counterpart's life and work, it wasn't feasible for us to link up because our lifestyles at that moment allowed no room for such. I know, I know . . . people make time for what they choose to make time for, and I agree with this statement wholeheartedly. However, some things are experienced, and some things get dictated. This entire journey for me operated on a hands-on approach. Learn as you go, Nichole. Contrary to what folks understand about this connection, the journey teaches you about learning from your past mistakes, forgiving yourself—whether it be the childhood or present you—elevating while refusing to remain in the same situations or circumstances that no longer serve your highest good, and knowing your worth.

## In the Beginning...

So, you see, yes, the love shared between two unique souls as one is experienced. However, there lies a lot more depth to this connection outside of the affection that is publicized between the parties involved that isn't focused on amongst the masses nearly as much as the obvious focal point of the intimacy between the DM and the DF. Thirty days had passed, and I couldn't believe how carefree this situationship was. There was no drama or headaches, so there were no issues on my end whatsoever. Even with the lack of physical interaction and me trying to look for a reason to end whatever this was I was involved in, I just couldn't honestly find a justified cause to let it go. Initially, I wasn't given a reason to. I was happy, and I had no complaints. Isn't that ultimately what matters? My happiness?

One of the strangest things to me about the connection was the attraction I had toward my counterpart. It was unmatched and untouched by another. The attraction wasn't what was strange; it was who he was on the surface that I was attracted to that made it weird. Under normal circumstances, I genuinely wouldn't have been drawn to him. Of course he's handsome, but he just wasn't "my type" and I wasn't his. It's funny because I recall telling him once that I wasn't his type, lol. Truth is, I'd never actually dealt with someone like him before, and in the past I wouldn't have. Please understand regardless how loving, nurturing, and caring I am, I have walls that I've built. My walls of trust and boundaries. Two years ago, these impenetrable walls stood one hundred feet tall and were made of titanium steel. I wasn't allowing anyone to enter due to past traumas I'd experienced in previous relationships. Prior to this journey, I was in an extremely toxic relationship with my youngest daughter's father. I learned sometime later while on the journey he was a karmic masculine, and usually you encounter a karmic or a false twin prior to meeting your actual twin flame. Somehow, with ease and poise, my masculine became one of the very few who got me to lower the drawbridge to allow him a chance to gain my heart. No funny shit. To this day, I joke about how if I knew then what I know now I would've kept at least two guards on site patrolling my heart. But everything happens the way it does for a divine purpose. My entire journey I had to lean on God's understanding and not my own. Many times, I was guided to accept things that I felt were unacceptable, forgive people for unforgiving actions taken against me, and love those who hated me the most.

## Chapter 3

# Drifting Down a Sea of Feelings

### Song: Regrets

### By: Jay-Z

Few people—rarely those who are familiar with the twin flame journey—speak on the dark night of the soul. Those who have, I will say I certainly appreciate the honesty about what I've read. On the twin flame journey, there comes a time when you experience this stage. It arrives without notice and literally causes a massive upheaval in the individual lives going through this. Seems like when this happened to me, it was one thing after another. My dark night of the soul was triggered by my Divine Masculine. The separation we shared—not being able to appreciate the little things that so many couples take for granted, like physical contact of any kind—started to take a toll on us both. However, the chemistry of our energy was so aligned those emotions didn't linger long. I just felt like everything was flowing naturally, so why complicate things by overthinking. To make matters worse, I was also dealing with a rather tumultuous situation involving my career, which was mentally draining and overwhelmingly stressed the fuck out of me. So much so that I ended up seeking therapy, searching for assistance in coping with the multitude of stress I was encountering that, to this very day, a resolution is still pending.

While traveling on my journey of the dark night of the soul, it did precisely what I believe it's intended to do for us all, which is to manifest an ego death. Both counterparts eventually experience this, but not necessarily at the same time. Certainly, the transition is contradictory to anything related to a harmonious experience. It's excruciatingly painful how it tests the very core of your true self. During the dark night of the soul, I was constantly submerged in challenging situations where I was forced to make difficult decisions that were in direct alignment to my connection. I dealt with the harsh opinions of the few people in my life who knew about my romance in whom I'd confided and trusted, only to slowly witness the confusion that started settling within them and the ridicule and sometimes harsh judgment I received as a response to their disapproval. How surprisingly flabbergasted I was when I learned some of the people I considered the closest to me were not in favor of the connection or the conditions of it. A few mocked me and this journey while others blatantly made their disapproval known every chance they could simply because they weren't able to resonate or relate to it. To them it sounded absurd and just impossible to mention, let alone believe.

I struggled severely for many days, during which I lost my passion and enjoyment for things I'd always loved. My ambition was depleted, and I felt like I was on autopilot. I wasn't living; I was existing. In a flash of a moment, feelings of joy that once resembled normalcy would vanish just as quick as they arrived with the very thought of my Divine Masculine. "What the fuck" was a statement I repeatedly blurted out to describe the agony and torture I felt during this ordeal I clearly had no control over whatsoever. I mean, truthfully, who would willingly stay trapped in this madness. I didn't want to be there. Unfortunately, there was no way out but through it, and my goodness, it was so dark . . .

The burden grew heavier as I was made aware of the reasons why those in my life disapproved. Mainly it was due to the mere fact that they just couldn't relate to it or the authenticity of what it represented: a soul connection. It failed to measure up to theirs and society's depiction of a "normal relationship." Funny thing though, no one has yet to enlighten me on just what that is. Although, one thing is for sure, and two things are for certain: It appeared that it wasn't what I had. It became clear that I left myself open to the criticisms of people by sharing my experience and was deeply saddened by the reactions I received in doing so. In the dark I couldn't understand why the opinions of others even affected me the way it did, but on the road to shadow work is where I discovered the truth of why it bothered me in the first place. Judgement is mostly what I encountered on this journey. Folks just couldn't fathom why I was so invested in this connection. I guess love was too cliché for them. Ironically, it was the only truthful response. I did it for love! More simply said, it was and remains my truth, so why wouldn't I? I inherited the strength and courage to proclaim my truth regardless of who understood it to be so or not. I knew God understood and that was enough for me. I promise you, there were moments when I would just break down and cry—not fully understanding what ignited this—only to discover that I am an Empath. I was receptive to everyone's emotions and I engaged with those feelings on a higher frequency. I didn't just sense someone's pain. I felt it. I swam in it, often almost drowning in other people's vibrations. I energetically experienced the emotions of others because of my love for God, humanity, the planet, animals, and other species of life, and it magnetized enormously. It is my belief that if you truly care for others, it will be evident in your actions and behavior toward them. Love is an action word. It can be proclaimed rapturously. However, without actions to coincide with the word, all it becomes is a word spoken instead of an emotion felt.

Sometime around November 2019, I began to question not so much the validity of my connection, but the integrity and lack of honesty my counterpart was displaying. As I began to feel more and more like Alice falling further and further down the hole in this journey, it became evident that I could no longer go to my loved ones for advice. I was guided to specific tarot readers, psychics, and spiritualists of light who assisted me along the charted waters I was sailing. Now, I'm aware many of my readers will roll their eyes in their heads at the mere mention of psychics. For the percentage of those who did that, please understand sir/ma'am that I am not here to convince you of anything, nor is my objective here to persuade you to think any way other than what's comfortable for you in your reality. However, this is MY TRUTH. So with that said, if discussions of supernatural things, spiritual encounters, and people with extraordinary gifts offend you, I suggest you read no further because I will be the first to tell you this book is going to disappoint you greatly. Shall we continue? Cool beans.

I embarked on this journey unsure of what I had gotten myself involved in, not knowing a damn thing about what this was, and more importantly not knowing how to navigate through it. My journey was sailed through the waves of the philosophical mindset of "You learn as you go." What has gotten me as far as I've reached has been nothing but God, love, hope, faith, and prayer. It was during the dark night of the soul I discovered the truth about Nichole. The road to shadow work was where I confronted her and where I learned the significance of this journey and the misconception of physical union being the primary factor of the connection. The more clarity I gained about myself, the more I also became aware of the circumstances that were occurring in my connection that the Spirit (Holy Spirit) would not allow me to ignore. Downloads began to come to me in the form of channeled messages in relation to my counterpart that I refused to tiptoe around. I began to understand the true significance of the series of events transpiring when they did and their direct contribution to me having an ego death.

Emotionally, the attachment I had to my counterpart was still apparent. However, there now existed a lack of truth and trust that replaced the love and integrity that had been established. So much so that I ended up coming across some information that was a confirmation directly related to the messages I had already received from the Spirit. When I asked my Divine Masculine about what had been brought to my attention, he immediately denied the information I brought to him. In fact, he downplayed my concern as if what I'd stated were false and required no more attention toward it. The concern I discovered was that he was in another relationship with someone else. He had no physical time for me, yet he'd managed to make time for another. Can you imagine the egg on my face? Even more disheartening was the fact that he wasn't trying to hide it. Love is blind, clearly, because I did not see any of these signs. But here was the truth now, right in my face in plain sight. Naturally, my heart sank and shattered into a million pieces. And there started the ego death. Can you imagine the pain, the humiliation, and the devastation I felt? Perhaps you can't, but as a Divine Feminine I was at my lowest point. All the plans I thought we were setting in motion for our future together suddenly felt like a facade. I felt played and I was angry and disappointed at myself for even having been in the situation to begin with. The opinions and criticisms of others regarding my connection began to haunt me and I felt embarrassed. Embarrassed for following my heart. Immediately I resonated with why so many chose not to keep their heart chakra open, the truth behind why people aren't vulnerable and why people eventually, after being hurt multiple times, give up on love altogether. Perhaps I could have swept the entire ordeal under the rug or brushed it off like water off a duck's back and just moved forward had I not been in love. But I was in love, and though you can fool other people and sometimes even lie to yourself about the truth regarding your feelings, you cannot fool your heart. The heart wants what it wants.

As I mustered the strength and courage to go to his social media accounts, the reality of how I was played for a fool and emotionally manipulated began to become more apparent. I couldn't deny what he had done. What I couldn't seem to understand was why. What the fuck was the point? There, in my face, was the evidence that he wasn't just dating someone else, but he was engaged to her. Wow! If there are any twins reading this, you know firsthand how devastating it is to discover that your love was manipulated and abused. I no longer gave a fuck what anyone had previously said to me about the connection because other people's opinions weren't what triggered the dark night of the soul to catapult me into doing the shadow work required to heal from this. It was the realization that I had to accept that, sure, my love was genuine but his wasn't—at least not from the lenses I was looking through. He clearly had ulterior motives and I was angry at myself for falling so hard—something I evaluated deeper when I arrived at the place of healing as I dived headfirst into dealing with my shadow work. I felt taken advantage of and played for a damn fool. I sensed that clearly none of this mattered to him. I didn't deserve to be treated the way I was treated. But I had also forgotten the lesson my dad and grandma taught me as a child, which is a person can and will only do to you what you allow. "Damn," I said. I know better. So, who was I more disappointed in then? Me or him? It's no secret I have an enormous heart and I love unconditionally and will do whatever I can to help those I love. Naturally, you could presume if my counterpart needed assistance financially, I was more than willing to help. Anything I ever do for anyone is always from the heart. However, I became upset when I started recapping all I did, gave, and invested into this connection. This was completely out of the ordinary for me. I didn't have a history of moving like this. Why was this able to happen? What was the fucking point? And why did I still love a man who did nothing but toy with my emotions?

Despite knowing the truth enough to walk away, I was still energetically tied to him. I tried to forget about him and the connection altogether but couldn't. It was like no matter how much I attempted to move forward, I somehow found myself always stuck swimming in a sea of emotions that I just couldn't regulate. I felt betrayed by the Universe and God and asked through countless tears,

"Why me, Lord? Why would you allow this man to do this to me?" See, it hits different when a breakup occurs and someone in the situation feels they were misled and taken advantage of. Trying to process what went wrong and why I didn't see the red flags from the start is a hard pill to digest. Under normal circumstances, I wouldn't have allowed myself to become so vulnerable to anyone, but I did, and it hurt. It hurt bad. I turned to the only thing I knew that could fix it for me. I turned to God. For me, I think what hurt the most wasn't what those who were aware of my pain were probably saying behind my back, but the betrayal, lies, and manipulation by my DM. See, when you're experiencing a dark night of the soul, some of your most disturbing, dark, suppressed thoughts come to the surface. You cannot escape yourself, even though people spend years trying to. This experience triggered all types of hurt and resentfulness that I wasn't consciously aware existed. Just when I would think I was past this bullshit, a day would always come that reminded me how much I wasn't. I consistently prayed for the strength and courage to face my pain and heal from this because it was slowly but surely eating at my essence. The dark night of the soul charges into your life to knock a chip off your shoulder that, in many cases, becomes bigger than the individual themselves.

My ego was crushed, while my self-worth went from assured to skeptical. I was irate and depressed all at the same time, trying desperately not to show it in the physical. Wasn't like I was trying to front like everything was OK;

I just refused to show emotions from that moment on due to trust issues. The way I saw it, being vulnerable caused me nothing but heartache. After a long period of isolation, tears, hurt, and sorrow, I guess I was ready for the next stage in my journey because, without any introduction given, a guide appeared to show me the route to take me to the world of shadow work. I was told this road wasn't smooth at all, and it wasn't an easy voyage or else everyone would travel it, but it was the surest way to healing and enlightenment . . . so I made my decision to take the path least traveled along this grim, dark, and gruesome road to the world of shadow work.

# Chapter 4

# When the Pain Outweighs the Pleasure

## Song: Sucker for Pain

### By: Imagine Dragons w/Lil Wayne, Wiz Khalifa, Logic, Ty Dolla $ign ft. X Ambassadors

Shadow work sounds exactly like what it is: work done on the darkest parts of your inner self. It's the suppressed elements of the self that one often buries within the subconscious thought of who they are versus who they project themselves to be to the world. Everyone's shadow work is different, as are we; but for the most part, we all share the sentiments of having to face some things in our past, or some toxicities in our life—past or present—that we refuse to confront. The phrase shadow work is derived from the term "the shadow self" accredited to 20th-century psychologist Carl Jung. It is explained as the unconscious part of the personality that the over-conscious ego doesn't want to identify. According to Jung, "Everyone carries a shadow and the less it is embodied in the individual's conscious life, the blacker and dense it is" (C. Jung).

Not everyone going through shadow work is comfortable sharing their experience with other people. There are various reasons for why that is. However, I believe the primary reason has a lot to do with the ego, which surprisingly is a dominant trait that the individual encountering this stage of the journey is trying to regulate. I, for one, had grown restless from countless nights of crying and pain that even when I tried to avoid confronting the darkest and deepest parts of me, I was no longer able to continue doing so. I was challenged to return to my past to get to the root of what had gotten me to the sunken place I was residing in. I became aware that there were unspoken things I was refusing to deal with that started resurfacing in my adult life. I wanted to understand why I kept attracting a series of repetitious events that began to feel like a never-ending story. The truth of the matter is I had to come to the realization that not every issue in my life was based on what "they" did to me, but, more often than I cared to admit, was equally rooted in self-sabotage as well. A wise person understands that surely it can't always be everyone else that is the problem. Sometimes we ourselves are the problem that needs to be fixed.

If you ask me, I believe the first rule of thumb traveling on the path of shadow work is accountability in the role one plays in their own demise. If you can't adhere to rule one, there is a strong probability that you won't complete the path, nor will you heal. It sounds quite simple, doesn't it? But let me assure you, thinking that way is far from accurate. Some of the core reasons it is so difficult to take accountability for one's contribution to a tower moment in their lives has everything to do with accepting responsibility for their own actions in the tower. As you become enlightened you begin to understand that there exists people (and I know because I have been these "people" in my life on several occasions) who would much rather place blame on everyone else but themselves. This type of mentality seeks sympathy more than empathy and pity versus compassion.

Initially, I began to reflect on how I felt about myself truthfully. See, on the surface all of us are guilty of giving off the appearance of "self-love," but it is our actions toward ourselves and what we accept that others do to us that truly determine how much we love ourselves, if some of us even love ourselves at all. Please understand that shadow work allows no room for delusions, illusions, or mask to be worn during this journey. Indeed, the primary reason for that is because it's counterproductive to the healing one is attempting to acquire on this path. Ironically, this is also the very reason why many people go years avoiding doing their shadow work. These individuals are often seen running from their true selves in life because there is something about themselves or an event that took place in their lives that they want to avoid confronting. It matters not whether this is done consciously or subconsciously because the effects and conclusion of both are the same.

There is a multitude of reasons for why that is. As individuals, these reasons for us all will differ, but we all share the commonality of trying to avoid the unavoidable. Like many before me, and I'm certain like many who will come after, would agree, the path to shadow work begins in revisiting your childhood and the traumas experienced that possibly you weren't even aware were traumas. I grew up as a kid in the 90s, an era when everything in the world seemed to be shifting toward something vibrant, unknown, and fresh. Quite naturally, music mirrored this energy, and like anything with a dominant influence, music quickly began to shape my lifestyle, the clothes I wore, the places I went, the things I did, and the people I interacted with.

Then and now, colorism and its existence seem to continue to have a heavy mastery within all sectors of life. This is a repetitive issue amongst the African-American community, where division and disparities are created within one's own ethnicity. For those of you reading who are less familiar with the term, colorism is defined as a form of discrimination or prejudice against another individual of the same shared race and ethnicity based on their melanin being darker. It honestly should be of no surprise that colorism dates back as far as slavery. Most of us are aware of the separation of classes based on melanin and how it was dictated according to the perception of those in power. Did we not have the house negro and the field negro conceptualization, in which lighter-skinned slaves were able to work in the big house and were afforded better living quarters, food, and clothing as opposed to the field negro who had to work in the field all day, was physically abused ten times more than their lighter-skinned brothers and sisters, slept in horrible conditions, while barely even getting scraps to eat? This very disparity amongst the shared race created somehow a sense of entitlement and notoriety by one fairer-skinned black over the other darker-skinned black. Yet in truth, both were still globally and economically oppressed and very much disadvantaged by the same powers that created a separation amongst the race from the very beginning through actions of "perks" like entitlements and prestige.

Perhaps I should remind you guys of the "brown paper bag" test that was orchestrated around the 1900s and used until about 1950. It became depicted as some level of acceptance or acknowledgment from white people in conceding who the "good Negroes" were and who weren't. I analyzed it as a form of societal approval and allowance created by white people in power to divide and conquer the races from within. Many churches, nightclubs, and fraternities used this "brown paper bag" technique as a test when allowing blacks to enter these establishments or receive certain types of employment, if employment at all. Despite all these events existing way before my time, somehow I also failed to escape the experience of colorism felt by my darker-skinned African-American ancestors during my own adolescence.

I'd be lying if I denied this definite truth that children can be quite cruel. They certainly lacked empathy for other children's feelings when I was growing up. I guess that's why my reaction to online bullying is sometimes jaded. Back in my day, as a kid you were told to stop tattle-telling on someone who'd made you uncomfortable or to just ignore them. It's amazing in this generation, however, these very same red flags have become clear indicators of abusive treatment. Yet during my childhood, these signs of perversion meant absolutely nothing at all to anyone but the person who was on the receiving end of the abuse. You never truly know just how cruel the world can be until you're the one being beat up by it. The safety and comfort of my home led me to believe in a world outside of my home that didn't align. I noticed the injustices placed on people, specifically African Americans, at a very early age. However, my home was still my security blanket for the times when the world just didn't make sense.

If you knew me as a child, you would certainly agree that I had a cheerful and sunny disposition that was accompanied by a charismatic personality that instantaneously caused people to gravitate toward me, some for good reasons and others not so much. Regardless, there was a light encompassing me that attracted a variety of people my direction. As a child it was difficult dealing with the harsh criticisms and the often mean words kids said to each other, but it hits different when an adult is contributing to a vicious cycle of verbal abuse that was shaming and teasing toward a child. I can't imagine not being affected mentally by an adult who contributes to teasing, badgering, and mocking a child for any reason—least of all the color of their skin—for simple shits and giggles. Yet it happened, and I am that child. All too often I recalled being made the object of people's jokes whenever us kids would link up on the block to kick it, and naturally its normal for kids to be kids to some extent and do what it is kids do. However, what wasn't normal was an adult participating in the theatrics.

I was not your overly emotional type of kid who was so supersensitive that I couldn't take a joke as good as the next person. But at some point, the constant jokes and the teasing began feeling less and less like kidding and more deliberately said and done with the intention to hurt my feelings. No longer was it "funny," like when we often laugh uncomfortably at ourselves in embarrassment. However, the ones who were doing it to me were the same people I'd considered as "my friends." Sadly, one of my childhood friend's mother, along with the rest of my circle of comrades, created this horrible name: They referred to me as Tarbie. It was said to emphasize on how skinny I was, like a Barbie doll, and my skin complexion, which was black as tar. While everyone just thought this was so hilarious, I was deeply emotionally and mentally affected by it. Nonetheless this "friend's" mother eventually began calling me this instead of my actual name, even though I made it clear I wasn't OK with the name, nor did I find it the least bit comical. Believe it or not, this behavior continued for years, well into my early twenties. Growing up, I just couldn't understand why people were always making fun of my skin complexion and the satisfaction it gave them to insult my complexion.

Colorism to this day still follows my trail, but I am no longer that defenseless child. I had to heal that part of me and remind my inner child to forgive myself because there wasn't anything wrong with my complexion. More importantly, I had to forgive the ignorance in people who hurt other people simply because they aren't happy within themselves and as a result often project their negative vibrations unto others. It was not OK how I was treated, and it was unacceptable then just as much as it's unacceptable now. The more I reevaluated how I was treated by those closest to me, the greater it became evident that somehow this situation affected me in ways I wasn't aware of due to suppressing the situation altogether while convincing myself as I got older it didn't affect me any longer. Unbeknownst to me, it most certainly did affect me in other ways in my life that, until I did the shadow work, I had failed to recognize had acted as a gateway to additional traumas.

All too often we as people suffer internally with uncomfortable pain, as we shy away from our truth because it is sometimes too awful to bear. However, when we decide to ignore the overall conditions that made us feel these emotions, the problem doesn't vanish. Many of us may have been raised in a household that was particular about what was discussed and whom it was discussed with. Should a topic of discussion create some form of stigma or unpleasantness, the topic wouldn't even come up. As an African-American woman, I couldn't tell you how many times I heard the expression "What goes on in my house stays in my house," or "You better not be talking my business to outsiders," encouraging children to grow up being silent about the terrible things that happened to them. No wonder according to the National Center for Biotechnology Information, depression rates are highest amongst black and brown people. Sometimes while growing up, male counterparts are taught that being a "man" means not showing emotions, signifying emotions are a form of weakness. These boys grow up being told men are defined by their strength, their dominance in power, and their ability to provide for their family. Being vulnerable, having sensitivity, and showing feelings, especially crying, are frowned upon and certainly weren't encouraged during my childhood era. Nonetheless these apathetic emotions can eventually, if left untreated, contribute to anxiety disorders, narcissistic traits, and possibly even masochism. After reexamining past childhood events while confronting some dark truths, I noticed how addressing these traumatic situations allowed me to understand my repressed emotions and their contribution to how I became a fragmented version of my true self. These steps I discovered apply to me specifically and are not a general conceptualization. There were three contributors that influenced the fragmented version of myself: insecurities, people pleasing, and an inflated/altered ego.

    I believe that a lack of self-empowerment and poor self-esteem can transmute into abusive behavior when authority is bestowed upon an individual in a separate area of their life that doesn't mirror the environment in which the individual would normally feel inadequate. Do we as human beings all have insecurities? Absolutely! Do we always address them in a healthy, constructive manner? Hell no! Insecurities and how they present themselves vary for everyone, as well as the influences that cause a person's insecurities. If you were to ask me, insecurities in the simplest of terms are rooted in one's fear to take a risk to try or do something unfamiliar while doubting their own ability to excel. We have all in our lives encountered a moment or two when we've felt insecure. However, the issue isn't feeling insecure momentarily. Rather, the issue concerns whether a person should allow these emotions of inadequacy to fester instead of allowing growth and change to influence a person's evolution as an individual.

As I examined my own moments of insecurity, I noticed those were the occasions when my desire to achieve more for myself or manifest a different outcome for my life that differed from what I had grown accustomed to was put to the test. The world we live in thrives off competitiveness in almost everything we do. Societal standards of what is considered "beautiful" have often left a disparity amongst groups of people who do not fit into the "prototype" of what defines beauty, and they are left with submerged feelings of inadequacy, unworthiness, and low self-esteem. I know, I know, nothing is absolute. So, for the individual reading this going, "That's not true, I don't see it that way," that's all well according to your perception on how you view this statement. However, for me the author in my perception,

## When the Pain Outweighs the Pleasure

I hope you are able to see things on a 360-degree and not solely from a 90-degree angle. #AlwaysRight ☺

The further I examined my own shadow work, the more I became illuminated to the subsequential correlation of the additional elements that participated in feeding my shadow self that I was repressing. The insecurities in my life I harbored opened the gateway for people pleasing, which instantly led me deeper and deeper down a dark hole of avoidance toward my own feelings, consequentially leaving me depressed and apprehensive. People pleasing as I interpret its definition describes an individual who adamantly puts the happiness of others before their own satisfaction and, oddly, often to the detriment of their own pursuit of happiness and personal fulfillment. In my experience, people pleasing was a tactic I often used as a coping mechanism to avoid confrontation, conflict, and drama, believing if I just went along to get along, it would restore balance to an agitated and tense situation.

On the contrary, it did the complete opposite and left me feeling unappreciated. I allowed myself to be taken advantage of and lacked regard for my own wants, but I guess it was presumed that was forfeited the moment I became a people pleaser. Typically, a people pleaser is someone who considers the wants and needs of all parties involved. If they are operating at a high-level frequency, these individuals are quite helpful, kind, and supportive to others. However, people pleasers vibrating at a lower frequency sacrifice themselves and their own contentment by apologizing for things that aren't their fault. They also base their self-worth on how others perceive them, and not necessarily on how they see themselves. People pleasers have this uncanny inability to say no. This failure to establish boundaries attracts narcissists and energy vampires who view them as pushovers. Eventually this behavior engages the individual, altering their personality depending on the company they keep and/or the audience surrounding them.

The ego, if it is functioning from a healthy, balanced conscious, preconscious, and unconscious mind, can be quite useful in social interactions, as it enhances self-confidence in one's worth and natural capabilities. However, if the ego becomes toxic and excessive, it will create an imbalance that, if ignored, will present itself in an individual as narcissistic traits and behaviors. Now, I am certain we as people have all had a moment of ego tripping once or twice in our lives. However, if you are a balanced soul, you will eventually check your ego before it grows out of control. Those who lack the grounded guidance of their higher selves to use their discernment to maintain humility and modesty will find themselves living a very superficial lifestyle that is full of exaggerated truths.

In my experience, the true personalities of people with inflated egos are a complete contradiction from the image they create and portray to the outside world. I believe that inflated egos derive from a fear of feeling and from believing that we are inadequate in some area of our lives. The inflated ego appears as a self-esteem booster, yet the esteem presented is nothing more than a false, generated persona. Inflated egos function from a requirement or need to be validated, accepted, and approved of by others in our personal lives and social groups, and a need for overall recognition in direct alignment to worldly success amongst our own family, peer groups, and co-workers. If you were to ask me, I would argue alter egos are created out of some sort of displacement and avoidance of the self and created by unhealed traumas that are still active in the psyche. Many celebrities invent alter egos for entertainment purposes. But I wonder about their ability to create and become a separate personality that differs from their authentic self, and more importantly, why they feel the need to make up an additional persona other than the self who they truly are.

Believe it or not, these inflated and altered egos that people incorporate into their personalities serve as a barrier of protection to some extent, or a wall of defense, that disallows people from knowing the "true them." Some have trust issues because their true selves were taken advantage of when they showed who they were. There are others who may feel as though their true self isn't acceptable today or by the targeted audience; they show themselves to be as it relates to their career. If these fragmented versions of the true self aren't examined and addressed with healing by practicing self-love instead of people pleasing, ultimately we will never know our worth or fully accept that we are more than enough. Instead, we will continue heeding our insecurities as we masquerade as everyone but our authentic selves.

## Chapter 5

# H.A.A.R.S.H.

## Song: Just Fine

## By: Mary J. Blige

So there I was, after coming out of the dark night of the soul, having addressed my shadow work, and now accompanied with an abundance of clarity for how and why I ended up at the exact moment where I was and the significant role it had in my twin flame journey. I was left with a souvenir in the form of an acronym to remind me of my travels. These six letters forever transformed my life from that moment on. H.A.A.R.S.H. stands for humility, accountability, abandonment, rejection, self-love, and healing. Each letter became another level of enlightenment that I needed to understand and master before I received clearance to elevate to the next stage. It makes total sense why humility was the first lesson learned.

*Humility* has a strange way of appearing in our lives during the least expected moments, yet somehow it leaves an everlasting impression. Humility can come into a person's life during a time when they are arrogant, self-serving, or lack empathy for the underprivileged and less fortunate. There are times when people, those of whom have been blessed with a wealthy lifestyle, often will conduct themselves in a pompous, entitled, and privileged manner. As a result, the universe gifts them with a lesson in the art of humbleness. I, on the other hand, wasn't wealthy, so I couldn't quite grasp why I had to go through a tutorial on humility. The lesson on humility that is encountered while on the twin flame journey differs for each person. However, collectively, we all experience being humbled on this journey.

My lesson in **humility** and the active role it played on this journey came without warning. I've always considered myself to be humble. However, my humility was tested in ways I couldn't imagine or prepare for. Humbleness is void of pride and ego, and my pride was shattered when I spoke of my journey to those closest to me. The reaction I received from many hurt my pride, and instead of focusing on this eternal and blissful love, my ego got the best of me to the point that I felt I had to prove that I was telling the truth. I do not think it was the journey necessarily that people (the small few I trusted to tell) didn't believe but more so who my twin was. It sounded too unbelievable to be true, but, hey, that's the twin flame journey for you. The humility for me was to experience a rare connection without the approval of family, friends, or society. This was the crossroads for me: Do I see it through to the end of the tunnel, or do I allow the 3D perceptions and opinions of others to dictate what my truth is? Are people's opinions about my truth more authentic than my absolute truth? I learned while traveling on the road to humility that no one is better than the next; some of us are presented with better opportunities, and with those opportunities we take risks to secure the life we desire for ourselves. For love, I sacrificed a lot. Growing up, I was raised with the understanding that love is a verb, so I express love in every way I can, beyond just merely saying it. The twins are each other's reflection, so everything I experienced, certainly my Divine Masculine also encountered. It was just not in the same way. My twin had to encounter his own lessons on these occurrences.

**Accountability** is such a sensitive topic for a lot of people to accept in their lives. There are folks who go years avoiding accountability for their actions while insinuating a victimized role in life, always to place the blame on everyone else but themselves. In society there aren't nearly as many people advocating accountability in their daily lives as people would lead you to believe, and this failure to take responsibility for a personal role in your own chaos is why you constantly have people repeating the same mistakes while avoiding and ignoring the culpability they share in the chaos. Did my Divine Masculine hurt my heart and feelings with lies and deceit? Yes. However, the truth is I gave him the green light to do it when I didn't establish boundaries. Had I done that from the beginning, a lot of things that hurt me could have been avoided. I also didn't take accountability for how I allowed certain things to happen to me just from failing to see past the rose-tinted glasses I was wearing. RED FLAGS should never be dismissed.

We have no control over what people do. However, we can control what we allow and accept to be done to us. Once I accepted accountability for my participation in allowing myself to be treated less than I deserved, I began to understand how an individual treats me begins and ends with me. People can only do to us what we allow. Accountability isn't a fan favorite amongst people because it places responsibility back on us for why we initially tolerated someone mistreating us. The truth of the matter is people are going to treat you how you treat yourself. Did I see the red flags? Absolutely. But like so many of us, I chose to ignore them and see only what I wanted to see and not the entire situation being presented to me. I realized my anger and disappointment was displaced. The expectations I had weren't warranted, nor were they reinforced with boundaries, so it would likely give the appearance that I was saying one thing yet accepting another. Yes, I had every right to be frustrated with him, but I needed to be equally frustrated with myself just the same for making poor decisions. Instead of wallowing in my pain, I chose to take accountability for where I went wrong and learned the lesson that I needed to learn. Everyone's lesson will be different, but the governing energy of accountability is what is achieved.

What I have experienced as applicable to my truth along the journey is, initially when most people are wronged, they have a wounded warrior sort of mentality (nine of wands for my tarot readers ☺) while failing to see fault in themselves. However, they see it clearly in the one who hurt them. I think the million-dollar question ultimately becomes, why did we allow ourselves to tolerate the behavior if we did. Accountability allowed me to reexamine myself. There is a saying that goes: when you point a finger at someone else, remember three are pointing right back at you.

My *abandonment* issues had begun to resurface along my journey, immediately after I was shunned by my Divine Masculine. Issues that had been suppressed since my adolescent days that I was not aware existed until I was triggered by his absence and this newfound relationship. Honestly, I didn't even recognize I was battling abandonment issues until the journey. Oddly, most people do not have a clue they are suffering from abandonment issues. There are several signs, however, that will allow a person to know if they are experiencing this themselves. An indication a person may be dealing with abandonment issues is shown when a person gives too much of themselves to individuals who lack reciprocity. These individuals are quick to please others at the expense of their own happiness. Most times this is done to avoid some form of confrontation. Other abandonment issues are formed from harboring jealousy in relationships of all sorts, whether platonic, family-oriented, or otherwise. It establishes a lack of trust in a partner's intentions while developing insecurities about the relationships created, leading to difficulty expressing intimacy emotionally and needing to control or be controlled by your partner. I didn't realize I was suffering from abandonment issues until the journey forced me to come face to face with my truth and the long-term effects of my issues on not just me but what I projected onto others I interacted with.

Over the years, I'd unfortunately developed a tendency of always spreading myself thin in situations where I was overextending my generosity to people who abused it. Many times, I gave more than I received from people. However, I somehow saw no problem in that, presuming I was simply treating people the same way I expected to be treated in return. It wasn't until I addressed my abandonment issues that it became clear that many of my issues stemmed from a fear of loneliness that began in my childhood when my mother and father divorced. Shortly afterward, my mother placed me in the care of the Administration for Children Services. Some people are way too perfect to resonate with this truth, but my insecurities at this low point in my unhealed life caused me to have jealous tendencies in my relationships. It was evident the relationships I had were mostly connections where the love wasn't reciprocated equally. I was giving way too much of myself at the expense of my own fair treatment—expecting my partner to see the value in who I was, all the while overlooking the true value of my own self-worth.

The lessons I learned coping with *rejection* and my memories of feeling excluded were by far the most difficult stage to journey through, hence the acronym H.A.A.R.S.H. We all have to, or will soon have to, deal with multiple forms of rejection within our lives. Rejection leaves no stone unturned and can be found in any relationship dynamic, career opportunity, and hobby—distributed out by family, friends, foes, and lovers alike. Unbeknownst to me, the way I used to deal with rejection in my youth served as a precursor to how I dealt with rejection as an adult. As a child, I experienced rejection specifically when my race and complexion were referenced. As I grew older, the rejection was still concentrated around my complexion and race, but it was my intelligence, my confidence, and my strength that was also being undermined See, back in the early 90s, dark-skinned girls weren't trending. If you were dark-skinned and popular, rest assured you had better been fly as fuck and had a face that was flawless. ☺. Nonetheless, boys when I was younger weren't lining up at my doorstep, and my mother house phone wasn't jumping off the hook for me. It appeared to me that chocolate girls didn't seem to be the fan favorite, so naturally, I encountered rejection and disappointment most of my teenage years.

Sometimes when we displace our emotions, we convince ourselves if enough time passes, the issues we have will eventually fade away and will cease to be an issue any longer. Life operates uniquely in its unpredictable and unorthodox approach as it administers out lessons that teach us just how misguided that is. My prayer is that someone will read this book to learn what these behaviors are in order to transmute this way of thinking. When I was removed from my home—court ordered under PINS (person in need of supervision) as a ward of the state—the rejection I thought I no longer felt surfaced in a gargantuan way. Nothing says rejection quite like your family turning you over to the Administration for Children Services. It was me and me alone (with God of course ☺). No sister, no dad, no mom, no grandma. Nobody. And that is how I felt at one point. Like a nobody that no one wanted. I believe the rejection was so prominent for me because the rejection was something that was unavoidable. I had to continue moving forward in life regardless, despite my feelings of being outcast. Whether I felt it was wrong or right, the outcome wasn't changing instantaneously, forcing me to learn to let go and let God. To go with the flow and accept what was in the moment.

I cannot speak for everyone and how they deal with rejection individually, but I can tell you about Nichole. When I was battling with rejection in my teenage years (1997-2001), I rebelled. It was a direct cause and effect of feeling rejected. It took years for me to get past this stage. In my perception, if no one wanted me around, no one had the right to tell me shit! It was just that simple. I built up an enormous wall that few were able to scale. Often, I would feel trapped in my emotions about things I knew I needed to discuss but just didn't. I was still carrying unlearned behaviors from my childhood about counselors and therapy, so I completely avoided the possibility that perhaps I could benefit tremendously if I talked to an objective person about how I felt. Unwarranted feelings of shame, inadequacies, and grief aligned themselves to my personality while my true self was being overcast and suppressed. This created a lot of blockages in my own personal growth and development because, for a very long time, I just didn't feel "good enough."

If you do not deal with rejection in a healthy manner, you might develop into an introvert who forfeits the opportunities that life presents due to fear of hearing the word "no." Know this: When you inherit a lack mentality frame of thinking, it will only limit and stagnate your growth. What we must understand is that there are things in life we do not have control over, and one must learn to accept these things based on the power we have to accept the things we cannot change. Rejection is unavoidable. We all encounter it. However, the way we handle rejection is directly related to our self-esteem, healing, and growth. There is an old saying I am sure you are quite familiar with that goes, "Rejection is God's protection." Our perception about rejection needs altering. Perhaps what is being withheld from us has more to do with divine timing than believing we aren't deserving of our dreams and desires. Reexamining the rejection I have experienced has taught me to be grateful for nos, and to trust in God to know what's best for me and not what I think is best for me. If God permits you to live long enough, you will testify to a rejection in your life that you later understood why something didn't happen for you the way you wanted it to happen for you when you wanted it to happen. Divine

Timing, as much as people do not like to hear this, is a critical factor in relation to alignments. I can recall all too well the days of being rejected for opportunities for advancement at places I've worked, and immediately I began to question my worth, contemplating whether I was, back to the "good enough" syndrome simply because I wasn't picked for something I'd sought to obtain. This very test repeated itself in my career and personal life several times until I learned the lesson as it was applicable to me and broke the karmic cycle of creating counterproductive thoughts. This journey taught me that if I did not heal and failed to address healthy techniques in dealing with displays of rejection, it would eventually affect how I viewed and accepted my own capabilities and self-worth.

If you choose to live life like that (free will), you can anticipate becoming an individual who will be held back by your own inner wounds. If you choose (free will) to remain stagnant in outdated paradigms because of a fear of the unknown, you will be trapping yourself off from your own happiness. I don't know about you, but I am not foreign to the fear of taking a risk. In my past, an inability to leave my comfort zone stagnated me and kept me from some amazing opportunities as a child. I declined or sometimes didn't even show up to auditions for certain specialized schools because I didn't feel confident enough to go. I was so paralyzed by the fear of rejection I wouldn't even try. There were many risks I declined to take simply because I second-guessed myself and whether I truly had what was in demand. I did, but the problem for a while was that I didn't know that I did. The lesson learned here was I was always enough, always sufficient yet humbly still a work in progress. What I had to learn was that the value of who Nichole is was never determined by the opinions of others, unless I believed what others said about me, and who knows me better than me other than God . . . I rest my case ☺.

**Self-love** is a very overused and overemphasized phrase that is widely recognized by many, yet few practice the **ACTION** of loving themselves. All too often folks fall victim to proclaiming the **ACT** of loving their self verbally, yet their actions demonstrate otherwise. None of us are above the moments when we weren't mastering self-love in our lives. Whether we admit it or not, the evidence of self-love appears in 3D in how we treat ourselves and how we allow others to treat us. Surprisingly, many of us grew up witnessing arrogance, narcissism, and egocentric behavior displayed in ways that confused us into believing these toxic traits were characteristics of self-love. Believe me, I was shocked as all hell when I traveled the dark night of the soul, and while doing my shadow work realized I had experienced moments in my life where self-love was null and void. I was flabbergasted and would have argued someone down had they told me I lacked self-love prior to doing the work on myself to see the truth in the statement. The ego, I tell you, is something else. My ego manifested in survival tactics . . . so in other words, it would do what was necessary to make sure its position remained relevant in my personality. I don't know about everyone else's ego, but before I learned how to check that MF that resides within me, I learned just how far things could spiral out of control fueled by the pride, illusions, and delusions that the ego often initiates and feeds.

My understanding of self-love is not a dictionary term, but its definition is based on what the phrase means to me. Self-love is the overall positive and healthy affection, care, protection, and nurturing one gives to their self, independent of any co-contributors. Across the world, beauty is represented very differently. In some regions, beauty is mostly emphasized by outer appearance. There are billion-dollar industries that exist and are profiting from the presentation of what is defined as beauty. As a little girl, it was second nature to associate makeup with beauty based on what I saw on television and in the "real world." It was extremely rare that a beautiful woman would be noted for her natural looks in the 80s and 90s. Even today, "natural" is often overshadowed by people appearing to "look natural" but still aren't living in their absolute truth. Arguably one could ask the million-dollar question, which is what constitutes natural? We would all have very varied viewpoints on this topic, I'm sure of it. Regardless, big businesses and beauty product corporations alike paint the narrative of what defines beauty according to their product they are marketing to you and me. I understand they are working in a very competitive industry; however, I see the way little girls and little boys view themselves and how the expansion of their self-esteem is directly related to whatever society promotes as beauty or the lack thereof.

*Self-love* is so much more than the image we present to the world. It's deeper than physical appearances, living a luxurious lifestyle, or accumulating wealth and becoming successful. You can obtain all these things and still lack self-love, because love of any sort is a feeling that cannot be replicated inauthentically. Self-love is an intimate relationship with yourself where you nurture, care for, and promote growth from within. Please be mindful of confusing self-love with superficial tactics such as what I previously mentioned. Unfortunately, many have, and many will continue to do so. A dead giveaway as to whether someone practices self-love or not lies in whether the individual in question exemplifies boundaries, honesty, self-respect, dignity, honor, discipline, and integrity. Anytime either one of these virtues is void in a situation, self-love is usually absent as well. A lack of self-love can also be demonstrated in the toxins we place into our bodies, through the promiscuous and dangerous ways we create relationships, and the codependent attachments we form to other people and things.

My lack of self-love was displayed in my tendency to not establish healthy boundaries, thus creating very uncomfortable scenarios in my life where I was left feeling used, betrayed, and taken advantage of. I am not discounting the fact that all those things may have existed. However, had I established firmer boundaries in my engagement with people, I may have been able to avoid feeling used, betrayed, and taken for granted. It begins and ends with us first. However, those who choose not to be accountable for their own role in their demise will lean more toward the role of playing victim. It's easier to just blame everyone else for an issue than it is to see our own involvement in the problem before it even became one. Additionally, I began to understand just how imperative it was to establish boundaries and to let go of expectations. There is nothing wrong with having standards. However, the moment we begin to expect others to behave like us and do things like we would do them is the moment we set ourselves up to be disappointed. As soon as I understood this, just like that, a door opened, and I was able to walk through it and leave. I learned the lesson of self-love by observing what self-love wasn't.

Well, after that, the only place left to go was to heal. **Healing** was the final stage in piecing together everything that I had encountered on the journey that brought ancient long-forgotten wounds to the surface that needed confronting and mending. Some of you may find this difficult to believe, but there are many unhealed souls occupying the planet. You could probably travel almost anywhere on Earth and discover people who practice various healing practices such as yoga, meditation, affirmations, and Reiki, just to name a few. Ironically, most Americans avoid healing because in order to heal, it requires removing the bandage over the wound. The pain must be confronted. It takes a very strong individual to remedy pain that has been suppressed, dismissed, and dissolved without becoming apathetic. Speaking from my own experience, I can recall many times concealing my pain by disassociating from myself and my reality through risky behaviors while I avoided the wounds, thinking that was a constructive form of healing.

Avoidance, sadly, is not a characteristic in sync with healing. After experiencing all that I've mentioned, I was left with two options: either address these issues head-on and move forward or suppress my truth while continuing to avoid the inevitable pain. Pain for many of us has become an emotion that majority of people try to ignore rather than confront. However, unhealed wounds eventually will create unhealthy behaviors and toxic lifestyles. Healing isn't an easy task or more people would be receptive to it. The hardest lesson for me to learn while healing was having to admit that I was concealing my suffering and preventing my own recovery by refusing to acknowledge the pain. My ability to deny that there was trauma I had not dealt with only created even more pain and suffering, creating more wounds. These wounds appeared in my emotions, my mental stability, my intimate encounters, and my spirituality.

Forgiveness is required in the healing process. If not for the other person, certainly for yourself. Harboring grudges and animosity poisons the essence of who we are made to be and transforms us to the worst version of ourselves.

## Chapter 6

# Spiritual Gifts/Spiritual Warfare

## Song: Never Would Have Made It

### By: Marvin Sapp

This is the chapter of the book I am definitely going to lose some people. I'm sure of it. Please note my experiences are just that, so I don't anticipate everyone who is reading this to resonate with my experience. Nonetheless, it's a prevalent part of my journey and my truth. To make no mention of such is against my mission and dishonors my truth. My truth is mine, as yours is yours. If I were to tell you that we all have psychic gifts and abilities, half of you reading this would surely agree. The remainder of you guys would most likely say you don't believe in psychics or psychic gifts. I am not here to convince you otherwise. The purpose of this book is to assist and guide twins on their journey and to tell the truth about this experience that conveys my twin flame journey in its entirety as it is applicable to my life. Being obedient to the Holy Spirit, I am consciously aware of all the criticism I may possibly encounter by sharing my truth with you. Trust and believe, if I wasn't comfortable with the adversity, you wouldn't be reading this book.

My gifts, which I am so appreciative to God for having, have been with me since I was a kid. Growing up, I can't say it was encouraged to announce my gifts publicly due to the era we lived in. I knew if I told people half the things I knew, saw, and felt, folks would automatically assume I was crazy or I was engaging in some form of dark magic. Just so we're clear, to each their own when it comes to what people do with their free will. That's their business. However, I will not participate in any forms of divination displeasing to my God. In other words, I do not partake in spell work or black magic. I am an alchemist. For those who are saying, "Well, you read tarot and that's against God," I encourage you to bring that point to him, not me. Every gift given to me came from God and it needs no defending. Should you feel some way about what I do with my life on my mission I suggest you take your gripe to the Big Boss upstairs. Good luck with all that. My ability as an alchemist allows me to manifest what I want in my life, and this comes from the power of God. I do not manipulate energies, nor do I participate in anything that goes against the will and consent of another person.

My personal relationship with the Most High is completely contradictory to such actions. Everything isn't for everybody. You've got to know your lane. That's not my lane! I've been a dreamer my entire life and have always been drawn to movies of fantasy. In fact, one of my all-time favorite movies ever is *The Never-Ending Story*, followed by films like *The Lord of the Rings*, *Willow*, the *Harry Potter* series, *The Witches*, *Hocus Pocus* and so forth and so on. The older I got, the more intuitive I became in which my senses were heightened much more than others in my environment. I could read a person's energy the moment they appeared before me without them ever opening their mouth. I noticed I was extremely receptive to the emotions of others, so much so that often my own energy would reflect their feelings. This actually still occurs. However, I have more control in balancing it out. Initially, it was all very confusing. I never felt like I fit in, and in order to "fit in" I couldn't be myself entirely. I just felt like there was more to life than what was being narrated to us. I was fascinated by life, people, and the unknown and had a connection to astrology at the age of nine. Linda Goodman's book on horoscopes was the first book I ever read regarding astrology and I've been hooked since. Unfortunately, we live in a very judgmental society, regardless of how democratic it presents itself, in which we single people out simply because they differ in some way not familiar to the majority.

I have loved God since I was made aware of who God is at a very young age. I was raised in the church, went to Sunday school, sang in the choir, was a member of the usher board, and was a Girl Scout. I was baptized twice in the church, and there is no confusion about who I belong to. However, as I got older and embraced my spiritual gifts, some of my sisters and brothers in Christ often looked disapprovingly at me as though I wasn't in the same body as them . . . or were we? I remained true to God and myself and went his way—the way in which he was leading my life, equipped with the Holy Spirit's guidance. It was a bold move most assuredly on my part, but a move that was my journey to travel.

I inherently have a sixth sense about things, which we in fact all possess. It's just a matter of being aligned with our higher self in order to tap into that frequency. Some are better than others at it, but we are all capable of developing this ability. I believe we all are created with an "inner knowing." You will find in life there are many programs (the matrix) to deter you from trusting your inner guidance and intuition, in which you're encouraged to rely primarily on other people and institutions in your life. I'd much rather place my faith in God. With all things considered, certainly I understand the fundamentals of establishing order and a government to oversee the well-being and interest of society. I'd just often debate on whether that is being accomplished, or has it simply been designed to mask an illusion that it is. I knew I was different, as we all are, but I realized my difference is grounded in an inability to conform to things most people never bother to analyze. I wasn't trying to be rebellious. I just found it difficult to not question things that I saw as questionable. I quickly realized because of my inquisitiveness I was being shunned and categorized by the inhabitants of this world. I began to feel very withdrawn from people, so I began to suppress my abilities, fearing further isolation. The qualities and characteristics of who I am made me happy to be me. Yet in the same breath, living under society's norms started causing me to feel anxious and unsure of myself, while forming a competitiveness that mirrored the environment I was in. After experiencing being secluded and singled out for being a dark-skinned girl, I just wanted to feel normalcy as a preteenager, so I pretended to be me, but not in its entirety, in order to fit the world's criteria on who I was supposed to be. Little did I know then, it mattered not whether I was my true self, shadow self, or hidden self. I would be singled out regardless, because of who I am, and who I belong to. I just wasn't created to "fit in." The confirmation of this has appeared throughout my life consistently.

During the initial stages of my journey my gifts enhanced tremendously. No longer were my abilities dormant, submerged in my subconscious, floating around aimlessly in the sea banks of my suppressed memories. My journey initiated the Great Awakening for me. When I was a little girl, my father would often say to me, "With great power comes great responsibilities"—an inspiring quote that for years I thought my dad made up, only to discover later in life the actual quote had been recited for ages. I recognized it immediately from Benjamin Park in *Spiderman*. However, the message was valid nonetheless. With spiritual gifts of any kind come a responsibility that, truthfully, not everyone will execute justly. Thankfully, I believe God knows all our hearts and intentions and, for this very reason, is particular about who he gives these abilities to. Consider the people you know who are in positions of power that abuse their authority. These are individuals who were more than likely given powers that were executed unethically, who demonstrated their ill intentions on what their objective was as an overseer. People grant people positions of authority, and we know just how corruptible that can become. So just imagine if spiritual gifts were arranged under the same premise. Precisely the reason why these gifts are bestowed upon those who are chosen by God . . . Those who inherit these gifts are entrusted to be responsible with them. However, we are flesh, and the flesh is weak. There will be individuals of light who turn dark and use their gifts for dark purposes. That's their choice, because we all have free will. However, things that are given for good that are misused always result in karmic consequences. Many people hear the phrase "spiritual warfare" and they do not always have a concrete understanding of what that entails. For everyone, the type of spiritual warfare one partakes in may differ. However, what's common for us all is the war. Not necessarily a physical altercation, although it can very well present itself as such, but mostly an unseen adversary in a confrontation of some kind. Spiritual warfare is best described from the Bible in Ephesians 6:12. It reads, "For our struggle is not against flesh and blood, but against the rulers, against the authorities, against the powers of this dark world and against the spiritual forces of evil in high places" (NIV). The spiritual gifts individuals like myself receive are designed to assist and equip us in war. War comes in all forms. In my personal observation of the general public, I have concluded that we live in a society that highlights the things in life that can logically be explained according to mankind's standards of what is feasible based on what can be proven tangibly. Surprisingly, if you are blessed to live long enough, you will learn to accept that not everything can "logically" be explained but can still occur. It's safe to say to some extent, we believe this to be true. Certainly we witness, believe, and see miracles happening in life, and we accept that phenomenon. Yet we would rather confine discussions of the counter role that deals with curses, dark magic, ill-intended manifestations, and ritualistic sacrifices as things that you see only in movies, or isn't real at all. I assure you both are very real.

My experience with spiritual warfare varied in many ways, even before I was on the twin flame journey. As a chosen one, forces against your mission and purpose don't wait until you wake up to attack you, but instead have been sending agents your way to throw you off course your entire life. Whether awake or not, if you're chosen, you will be attacked. It's best you're awake and alert in my opinion than comatose to deal with your enemies and adversaries. Spiritual warfare for me often presented itself through the people I knew, the places I worked, and the institutions I was intertwined with. The closer I got to my purpose, the more I was attacked. People often get used as hosts and sometimes are not even aware they are being used as a ploy to attack a divine person. When someone operates from a low frequency (for example, envy, jealousy, or hate), unbeknownst to the individual being used, fueled, and controlled by dark forces, it allows them to assist in attacking another person unjustifiably in some way. These people are being energy-harvested by energy vampires who are basically contributing to helping them in targeting you, to witness your demise in some form. Whether consciously aware or not, the moment you proceed to operate out of a low frequency of toxicities in thought and deed, you subject yourself to forces and energies you may not be aware of that will begin to influence your motives, behaviors, and actions toward others and yourself negatively. As a result of fighting the good fight, I've lost some people, relationships, belongings, and even battles, but I never lost the war or the victory, because that belongs to God! Shit, I recently lost a side tooth as well with the battles I have fought in this spiritual warfare with people conjuring up black magic and spell work against me. It's fine, it's a tooth. Better that then my life, and that is what they were attempting to take. A tooth can be replaced, the Holy Spirit reminded me, but not me; I'm irreplaceable. No matter the attacks, or who my attackers were (and they were many), I continued persevering toward victory. I am blessed and grateful to say no weapons formed against me prospered. Psalm 105: 14–15 says, "He permitted no one to do them wrong, Yes, He rebuked kings for their sakes, saying 'Do not touch my anointed ones and do my prophets no harm.'" Attacks like these are always generated from karmic energies.

## Chapter 7

# Karmics

### Song: Rumors
### By: Timex Social Club

I'm sure many of you reading my book are familiar with the term "karma." However, the word "karmic" was known by mostly tarot readers, spiritualists, practitioners, and the collectives until 2020. Karmics are people and situations that have the sole intent of teaching you a valuable life lesson that will catapult you toward your highest self. When it comes to these particular people, karmics can be diabolical, causing nefarious acts of all sorts. They are emotional manipulators known for shape-shifting to fit a narrative that produces their intended results. That might not sound negative, but I assure you it is when you are dealing with people who will do anything to win (5 of swords energy for my tarot community). These people will lie, cheat, steal, and in some instances place spell work on others with a motive to harm innocent people for the sole intent of getting what they want. Karmics are known for manipulating people's free will in order to satisfy their own desires. All of us at some level have been karmic in nature, and all of us encounter karmic relationships. Karmic relationships are toxic, volatile, unhealthy connections usually formed from trauma bonds established between people. Karmics are superficial, egotistical, and self-absorbed individuals who harvest off other people's energy for their own selfish gains. Karmic relationships can include lovers, friends, family members, and co-workers. We have all encountered karmics and, to some extent, have all displayed karmic behaviors. However, no one has to remain on this frequency. People choose to stay low-vibrational and toxic. If you willfully chose to ignore and overlook your dark ways while catering to lower vibrations and messy toxicities, you then subject yourself to a never-ending story of karmic cycles. There is no escaping karma. She has everyone's address, both listed and unlisted alike.

While on my journey, the number of karmics I was attacked by was surreal. Many were strangers, and others were people I either knew most of my life or people I worked with. The people I knew for years collaborated with these strangers with a motive to inflict pain on me in any way possible. I experienced financial setbacks and hardships, emotional pain, and my physical and mental health was disrupted overall. My children even were affected by the nasty actions I was subjected to, by individuals I worked with. I experienced some of the worst trauma one could imagine. Knowing that this was intentionally done to me hurt more than the actual agony I faced. Through and through, God held me in his right hand and sheltered me while vindicating me in the process.

These karmic frenemies, karmic family members, karmic co-workers, and karmics who were attached to my DM all wanted one thing: to destroy me. Whether it was done by keeping me blackballed in a job position I was overqualified for—as I was repeatedly stagnated with a lack of growth opportunities—or former friends who were secretly envious of me, who took unjust actions toward me out of malice and hate, all of this was unwarranted. There were family members that I'd confided in who took my intimate secrets and exposed them in an attempt to ridicule and embarrass me while orchestrating weird alliances with secret societies and covens. You name it, I was experiencing it. Between the rumors and lies, it got so overwhelming that I began to isolate myself even further. I felt like I couldn't trust anyone but God. Truthfully, I can't! The closest ones to me had hurt me the most.

Karmics are extremely delusional individuals who envy others simply because they see characteristics in people they don't see in themselves, and this irritates them. My light is bright, and even before knowing this, I was told this by a karmic I work with. At the time I didn't quite understand what it meant, but over the course of my journey I learned. Out of all the karmics I'd dealt with on this journey, none were more diabolical than the karmics who were associated with my DM. He was surrounded by evil, demonic people who went to great lengths to sabotage the connection. These people knew of our twin flame journey before either one of us did. They, like my former friend, and my DM's ex (who too is a karmic), looked up our birth charts and learned about who I am and the role I played in my DM's life. They immediately went to work on ruining the connection out of pure hatred and jealousy. They knew I was spiritually gifted, but they didn't believe that I would stand in my truth. In fact, a prominent reason they even did this was because they felt they could get away with it. They sized me up and told themselves I wasn't anybody special and believed with conviction they would never get caught. It's the audacity and arrogance that had me in awe, as though they were more powerful than God. Sadly, these people tried to play God and ultimately got dealt with by God for the role they played. They were warned several times to stop what they were doing but took no heed. They were all operating out of ego. Ego that is unbalanced is dangerous for the participant and those closest to them.

Believe it or not, this community of people went as far as to hire practitioners to place spell work on my DM and me. Unbeknownst to him, they were already placing spell work on my DM and had been for some time. My DM's loyalty was manipulated against him, which caused him to be susceptible to the dark magic. Heavy mind control was placed on him through his food, his drinks, and the women he interacted with sexually. Plainly said, he trusted the wrong people and felt obligated because of his loyalty to stay amongst thieves and liars. Eventually he became the people who was surrounded around him the most. Karmics in our lives are co-dependent on us and are extremely jealous of our success. They are often seen smiling and celebrating with you like they had your best interests at heart, yet behind the veil, they despise you and secretly wish to be you. Truth is, they couldn't care less about you. They are concerned about themselves and how they can benefit off you and your success or your own demise.

Through sex, lies, drugs, negative influences, and other forms of toxicities your mind can be manipulated and controlled by these individuals, which results in you giving up your power. Karmics are concerned more about their own best interest. I, being a highly intuitive psychic and lightworker, realized quickly what the truth was behind closed doors and attempted to protect my DM by informing him of what was occurring. However, that too was manipulated by these minions and flying monkeys. The truth is, karmics had been manipulating him for years, way before I even knew him. As a clairvoyant, they knew hidden truths would be seen by me, and it would disrupt the order they already had established, so my presence was a threat. So much so that spell work was being initiated to trap his mind. The Holy Spirit would reveal these truths to me in variations of downloads in my dreams and other unique tactics. I didn't want to see what I saw, but once you see, you cannot unsee. I saw the lies, the manipulations, the control, and the plot to keep us apart. It pained me, more so because I was being attacked by people I didn't know or hadn't done anything to. Many nights I asked God, "But why?" He always responded the same. "My child, it's because you are you, and don't ever stop being YOU! YOU ARE MINE!" I cried many nights because, contrary to what this world believes about the twin flame journey, I didn't ask for this. I didn't seek my masculine. This journey found me, and it has been one of the most difficult journeys to experience. I prayed for God to remove it, including the feelings I had for my masculine, but the journey remained, as did the love.

Karmics are people with unhealed souls. They envy people who they secretly admire but are frustrated with themselves for not demonstrating similar characteristics within—the very attributes they find admirable in another. They can either remain karmics throughout life or they can heal, but often you will find they choose to remain as karmics. The reasons for that are different for every karmic. However, there are some major contributors to why they choose to be karmic.

1. It's a generational curse. This is the most common reason. Karmics who fit this narrative have an extensive history with negativity in their lives and the lives of their loved ones. Whether it's a particular lifestyle, upbringing, childhood trauma, mindset, practice, or known affiliations, healing seldomly occurs in the dynamic, thus allowing karmic cycles to continue repeating each generation until someone in the bloodline breaks the chain of these strongholds. Due to the longevity of the karmic cycles, you will find more

people in the family dynamic who gravitate toward their lower vibrational frequencies instead of their higher, and ultimately pass these behaviors to the future lineage. I believe we all have generational curses attached to us. However, not all of us choose to do the work to heal our bloodline. That's what makes it karmic.

2. Another popular reason karmics remain toxic is because they simply do not want to do the work. The work on the self depends on just how much work needs to be applied, and since it's an individual job, some have more work to do than others. When an individual consciously understands their errors, yet continually engages in the same destructive energy, I believe your very essence and inner light begins to rot and darken. Should it get to that extent, one just becomes comfortable and numb to the destruction and subconsciously embraces it as a form of familiarity regardless of the negative consequences it produces. It just becomes what they know! Their norm! So, its who they become! Of course, at any time they can disengage from this way of life, but the longer they sit in quicksand, the harder it is to get out of it. And should you attempt to escape, it will require work. Desiring change is one thing, but without the action supporting your wants, your desires just remain in park.

3. No matter how much we aspire to see the positive in all things, never become disillusioned to the

truth that evil does exists. There are many karmics who will not change because they willingly accept themselves as who they are or have become. There exist no plans of reform or repentance of any kind. They understand their assignments, as do lightworkers, and they operate throughout life fully aware of the diabolical schemes they inflict on others and society at large. These karmics don't appear as obvious in your life when you first encounter them, which makes them more dangerous. They are camouflaged in your lives as friends, family, significant others, and business associates who "appear" to have your best interests at heart. Many karmics that come into our lives succeed because they gained access to us through an over-inflated ego. When our ego isn't balanced, the enemy can infiltrate our camp through convincing forms of flattery and gaslighting tactics. Karmics are sent in your life to teach you a lesson, mostly about yourself! The intensity of karmic behaviors is measured by each karmic individual because they differ, and their karmic cycles are subjective. Karmics who choose to engage in toxicities with no form of regret or a willingness to grow and evolve tend to practice dark arts, manipulate magic, and place incantations and sorcery upon others to accomplish a gain of some kind. The gain varies from karmic to karmic, but the majority of them at this level engage in this activity with an intent to gain wealth, success, fame, or a particular public status. These karmics are the ones who also know about the twin flame journey—the DM and the DF— and they, along with their minions, go to great lengths to sabotage the union. Without discernment on this journey, it is easy to get caught in the matrix, as things often appear one way but are something else instead. Karmic actions—through various forms of manipulation, smoke screens, dark magic, and other lower forms of manifestation—create portals to try to avoid judgement each generation as they pass on these teachings to their lineage.

Sadly, I have encountered all the karmics mentioned. It breaks my heart when these karmics appear as friends and family. If you resonate with me, you probably expect people who don't know you to draw assumptions about you under false pretense because, hey, that's what people do right? However, when it's the ones around you who claim to love and support you who backstab and plot to hurt you is when for me it hits different. That's the epitome of betrayal. Karmics are nefarious in betrayals of all kinds. They lack loyalty to anyone or anything truly, including themselves. Yes, you read that correctly. They aren't even loyal to themselves, and for several of you, I heard you say "Huh." But when you are living behind a mask, you aren't living your truth, which means you are presumably disloyal to yourself. How can you legitimately expect an individual to keep it real with you who doesn't even keep it real with themselves?

If you are wondering how to identify who is karmic in your life, or if you're reading this and you're contemplating whether you are a karmic, here are some sure signs that someone connected to you, or you yourself, may be karmic.

1. Your motives are based on your gain solely and you don't have a problem hurting others to accomplish your goal.
2. You rely on manipulative tactics and mind control to assist in accomplishing your desires.
3. You are motivated by power, not passion.
4. Everything is a competition, and you must win at all costs.
4. You are selfish, narcissistic, egotistical, and self-absorbed.
5. You involve yourself with tasks that are self-serving.
6. You are willing to make oaths and deals to ensure and override your will over others.
7. You do not love others, but you gaslight people by telling them you do.
8. Your actions never match what you say.
9. You and your choice of peers are extremely superficial, and materialistic, who judge people based on social class and status.

10. You are extremely jealous of others, overcontrolling, and secretly insecure.

11. You are threatened by the success of others.

12. You are a damaged, unhealed soul. Should you notice these traits in yourself or someone connected to you, chances are you or they are karmic or karmic-influenced. But they don't have to remain that way... Remember they/you choose too!

Regardless, karmics, whether they choose to change or don't, are all responsible for karmic debt. "What you reap is what you sow," or my favorite, "As above so below." Karmics must clear their debt incurred. When they don't, it transfers over to another lifetime or passes along the family bloodline of a new generation. Karmic debt is all the toxic, low-vibrational traits and tactics that aren't healed. The accumulation of debt differs from person to person, but collectively the endgame is to heal or remain unbalanced with negative attachments to yourself and/or your lineage.

## Chapter 8

# False Flames

### Song: Triggered
### By: Jhene Aiko

On this journey, you will encounter all types of beings. You can come across shapeshifters, Ascending Masters, extraterrestrials, spiritual entities, various enemies, karmics, witches, angels, and deities of all sorts. Discernment is critical on this path because everything and everyone aren't always who and what they appear in your life to be. Shapeshifters, karmics, and succubus spirits appear completely contradictory to who they project themselves as in the matrix. These entities can resemble strangers or cloak themselves as your family members and friends. This is strategically done to gain their prey's (because that's how they look at you) trust and loyalty, in order to lure them away from their hedge of protection, smack dead into the devil's playground before they understand where they are, who they are with, how they got there, and what has transpired.

If you are part of the rare chosen souls on the twin flame journey, I can assure that you will encounter a false flame before you meet your actual twin. Don't ask me why, but every twin encounters this relationship. My guess is they are sent in your life to prepare you for your actual twin. It is quite easy to get caught up initially with a false flame because of the intensity of the affair you share with this individual. This bond can confuse a lot of collectives if they're not taking heed of the red flags associated with this false flame connection. False flames are karmic in nature. However, the role they play in this journey is to force you to set boundaries to make self-love a priority and to address and take accountability for your toxicities and destructive behavior. For those of you who are like, "I don't have toxic and destructive behaviors," sure you do, and the mere fact that you believe you don't will ignite karmic relationships into your life. False flames and other soul ties vary in the destruction they create in your life, but make no mistake, they come into your life and cause havoc. See, the problem is they don't arrive problematic. In fact, they pretty much show up as just what you're looking for—or so you think! Your twin in most cases is the opposite of your normal dating preferences. For example, if you're a man who dates a particular type of female, whether it be nationality, size, height, profession, etc., and that's the sort of women you attract, your twin will be the opposite of your usual type. It will defy logic because you will tell yourself, "Of course I know what I like, right?" Or do you? Perhaps the higher self knows otherwise. Should you be a twin and find yourself attracted to someone you most likely would probably not date, no matter how much your mind tells you it makes no sense, or the person isn't even your type, the higher self knows differently, and the soul recognition becomes activated.

One prominent difference between a false flame and a twin flame is you can have several false flames, but you will have only one twin flame. The reason we continue to encounter multiple false flames is because we do not learn the lessons we are supposed to while involved with the false flame, and we ultimately attract the same lesson to be learned, just in a different person. Hence, why some people continue to attract the same type of low-vibrational people and later ask, "Why do I keep getting the same type of relationships?" It's simple. There is something we need to discern about ourselves that we aren't consciously aware of when in toxic relationships that continues a cycle of dating different people with the same characteristics. Typical false flames are narcissistic, egotistical souls who pride themselves on keeping you unsure of yourself and your own potential. They have a condescending method of projecting feelings of inadequacy to the people they are in relationships with, as if they aren't good enough. They can have you feeling unappreciated, undervalued, frightened, and depressed. The longer you stay with this false flame, the more you begin to doubt your worth, creating low self-esteem and a codependency to remain in a loveless, toxic connection. If you remain there even longer than that, you can start to mimic Stockholm syndrome behaviors where you begin to accept the unhealthy connection as normal and even start to become tolerant to the toxicities involved.

When the false flame comes into your life initially, it seems so perfect. Everything appears to be going great, that is until time passes and you notice how the false flame influences or contributes to enhancing your shadow side. Maybe you used to be a social drinker before you met this person, but you find yourself lately becoming more familiarized with your neighborhood liquor store since dating the false flame. False flames fixate on aesthetics of all kinds but will try to avoid responsibilities as much as possible. They will indulge in toxicities with you, yet they won't participate in activities that enhance your growth, whether spiritually, academically, or personally. They will, however, support anything that involves monetary gain, especially if they see themselves getting a percentage of whatever you receive.

Many people have been under a false narrative about the twin flame journey. These people assume because they heard the journey is a difficult one to go through, the counterpart they are with is automatically their Divine Masculine/Divine Feminine because the relationship they share with their current counterpart is a tumultuous connection. Please understand, if someone you are in a relationship with is gaslighting you, abusing you in any form, is extremely controlling, or is jealous, violent, and treats you condescendingly, that person is neither a Divine Masculine nor Divine Feminine. The problem with many of us is our pride disallows us from recognizing the red flags that exist in toxic connections from the beginning. It's not that we didn't see them, honestly. We just chose to overlook them or blatantly ignored them altogether.

My experience with a false flame is they are extremely charismatic and convincing, but their actions do not coincide with what they say. They create false promises and use this ploy to play on your emotions. Initially, they act like the perfect partner, but the emphasis is on "act" because that is exactly what they are doing. No amount of acting will camouflage their true motives and identity for long, which are the red flags I was referring to earlier. Eventually you will notice a side of them that you don't recognize or didn't see in the past. Contrary to what our mind tells us, it was always there. It was just cloaked very well by keeping us fixated on how "too good to be true" the relationship is. These false flames live their lives behind masks, pretending to be someone they believe their victim desires. Then, as soon as they feel they've got the victim comfortable enough, they reintroduce themselves as their authentic form and all hell breaks loose. These people are extremely manipulative; they are thieves, liars, cheaters, and in some instances physically abusive to their counterpart, as they use various control mechanisms to keep their victim with them. The most notorious method is to attack their victim's self-confidence, making them feel inferior to other people. This builds a codependency bond and unhealthy attachment to a toxic connection, while creating fear that you won't attract better and a belief that you don't deserve better as a result of being brainwashed to believe you aren't better.

The false flame will continue to do to you what you ultimately allow and that is the hardest lesson to learn. If you do not set boundaries, love yourself first to recognize when love spoken isn't equivalent to the love shown, and learn to walk away from people and things that no longer serve your highest good, you will be just as much at fault for the chaos repeating in your life as the false flame. It begins and ends with you! You must heal the wounds within that made you feel comfortable to allow yourself to be subjected to this kind of treatment. Ask yourself, "Why am I tolerating this? Do I believe this is love, and if so, why is that? Do I love even myself?" The answers you receive can be mind-boggling. However, if you want to avoid these types of relationships in the future, you must first learn why this type of relationship was acceptable by your standards to begin with. Healing doesn't happen overnight, but like anything in life, persistence is the key to progress. False flames appear both to the Divine Masculine and Divine Feminine, and often they don't figure out how far down the rabbit hole they have fallen until they hit rock bottom. False flames, which I see as high-level karmics, bring curses and loss into your life. They have negative attachments they project to anyone they establish a bond to that keeps the people around them in a low vibration. Mental instability and depression are often developed as a result of being devoted to these people. In the words of Jordan Peele's 2017 thriller, my suggestion is simple: "Get Out" and do it quickly.

## Chapter 9

# Speaking Truth Unapologetically

## Song: What About Your Friends
## By: TLC

We live in a society where it's not uncommon to hear the phrase "Being my authentic self" proclaimed just about everywhere. However, it's not as common to witness people speak their raw unadulterated truth. In my opinion, truth has been diluted to fit a particular narrative that is not always a reflection of accuracy, facts, and honesty. Instead, I have witnessed alleged "truths" that were nothing more than fabricated, overly exaggerated tales. Truth today gives a jaded appearance of realism but is often masked by staged versions of authenticity and illusions fueled by an obsession with image and a need for attention. I have noticed that if truth deals with topics that aren't as popular and are discussed by people who aren't as popular, it tends to become overshadowed and either dismissed, robbed, or reiterated as a more known person's narrative and not the originator's. Throughout history there have been some truths that have made others so uncomfortable that they've become censored and often hidden from societies for decades and even hundreds and thousands of years. I, being a woman of integrity and truth first, knew in the early stages of this journey I would be severely criticized for boldly sharing my truth; however, I understood my assignment. Though I was walking this path individually, the lessons and teachings experienced during my journey were orchestrated to assist the collectives on their journey, and they need to be shared.

I chose to share my truth using a variety of methods even before I started writing this book. Initially, I shared my truth about my twin flame journey with a few select family and friends whom I trusted. My truth was judged harshly by people closest to me who didn't understand what this connection is. Then I spoke about it periodically on my podcast, (Co_cain-kiss33s) as I was guided to. Many of the topics I discussed related to the twin flame journey may have invoked a lot of skepticism and doubt from my listeners, but I talked about my experience nonetheless. Topics about black magic, demons, angels, and extraterrestrial beings are taboo for some and an acquired taste for others. Yet, it is far from being discussed as candidly as more popular and accepted subjects.

Speaking my truth came with consequences. I was ridiculed and gang-stalked on various social media platforms, as well as my devices were hacked. On my podcast I accumulated listeners from all over the world, and I shared my truth about the twin flame journey openly and honestly. Not everyone appreciates truth, especially if the truth begins to expose the fraudulence in them. So, those who were triggered by my truth began to use their resources in an attempt to silence me, but I wasn't created to be silent. I was created to tell the truth and shame the devil. I had frenemies attaching themselves to my trademark brand, causing me to have to reach out to my lawyer to address the legality of what they were doing. It was clear she wasn't working by herself. I had to also hire a computer software professional to run a diagnosis on my devices only to learn my phone was breached and compromised. The company CEO I hired called me personally to inform me that my device was hacked at a level of sophistication that he couldn't even touch. It was at this moment I began to realize just how invested people were in trying to destroy me. I gave his number to my lawyer and my lawyer called me back informing me that he'd spoken to the CEO of the software company. Though he'd had doubts about some of the things I was telling him, he knows now, as a Christian man himself, that I was telling the truth and I was vindicated.

Immediately my lawyer went to work, and so did I. Of course, the closer you get to the doors of truth, the heavier the opposition becomes that you face. I knew that people were betting against me defending myself and speaking my truth because, in their perspective, I didn't have the resources they had to prove what had been done to me. Oh but God…...!!! I had the best resource known to mankind: God, and my Father is a God of righteousness and justice. I was steadfast in the face of challenges and my adversaries. My strength comes from the Highest, and regardless of what was being done to me, I never backed down. I took some hits, but I am resilient and kept fighting. See, when you're in your purpose that God aligned for your life, nothing can stop God's will, no matter how much interference occurs.

I witnessed people stealing my creative ideas and content and adopt it as theirs. I called every single person out too that I noticed doing that, from average joes to famous people you would never suspect would be that trifling. Who they were mattered not to me, nor their status in life. If you steal from me, I'm airing you out. It's just that simple. I've worked too hard for everything I have and got it out the mud, so it pains me when people copy me, my work, and my content, then masquerade it as their own. There's no honor or integrity in that, and all things done in the dark eventually come to light. Throughout my journey I've witnessed people of all races, demographics, and walks of life advocate authenticity who were far from demonstrating the definition of the word in their deeds. How can anyone be considered authentic living behind a mask? I am a free spirit and will always live in my truth, whether good, bad, or indifferent. I don't paint narratives based on popularity, trending topics, clout, money, success, or any other superficial reasons for attention. My truth is simply that, and it is far from perfect, but it's honest and no one's tale but mine to tell.

The truth about the Divine Masculine is the DM isn't always awakened to the journey. It is the Divine Feminine who wakes up their counterpart, and it's the DM who learns how to navigate through these uncharted waters from the DF. Please understand, not every DM operates the same. However, many share the same behaviors and traits. My DM knew about this journey and who I am to him. However, he was comfortable living in the past. He was too stubborn to change and just didn't want to do the work to elevate to his higher self. He saw the journey as difficult and confrontational, and it forced him to make alterations to his life that he wasn't ready to do. Did he know his life was full of toxicities? Absolutely, but it was the only life he knew. He was afraid to change and to take a risk toward something else, something unknown.

Many Divine Masculine's are surrounded by disloyal people, including and not limited to their own family members. A lot of people are codependent on the DM, and the DMs are used by those closest to them. They don't speak up for themselves because they hate confrontation and instead go through life as people pleasers, never pleasing first themselves. Unfortunately, they are often placed under various forms of manipulation and operate through much of life on autopilot. They have severe trust issues and deeply rooted childhood traumas. In some cases, they even assist in trying to destroy their own counterpart. Sounds karmic, doesn't it? There is healing that needs to be done, but they avoid healing by substituting it for numbing mechanisms, like drugs, sex, and other forms of toxic alternatives. The DM is highly spiritual, and just like their counterpart, they inherited spiritual gifts also. But unlike the DF, they use their gifts for low-vibrational activities. They usually become triggered by the truth spoken by their counterpart, and if they're like my DM, they can collaborate with others to attempt to silence the DF. The bond cannot be denied or ignored, yet they try like hell to. The connection forces them to look at the truth in who they are and have become. Two of the biggest mistakes DMs make is the same mistakes the DF makes along the journey. The DM seeks advice and the opinions of other people when they already know what they feel. They seek validation from people. The agents in their lives know this about them, so they purposely give them bad advice, knowing that the DM will adhere to what they are told and will end up keeping themselves stuck while everyone else around them is fulfilled off their hard work and unhappiness. The second mistake both counterparts make is they try to change the other to fit their narrative of what they want them to be instead of loving the individual unconditionally for who they are. It isn't anyone job to change another. The change comes from the acceptance of the individual to want to change and God will.

The DFs go through a lot. They fight countless battles both spiritually and in the 3D (not literally but can be for some). They do the work on themselves and build an intimate relationship with the Divine, who assists them every step of the way on this journey. They learn about their mission, their purpose, and their Ascending Masters who accompany them on the journey. They learn more about who they truly are. It is far from easy being a DF. For those claiming to be a Divine Feminine reading this and you haven't been chosen or you haven't done the "work," I most assuredly wouldn't keep running with that narrative if you aren't ready to accept everything that comes the Divine Feminine way—good, bad, and indifferent. Precisely the reason everything isn't for everyone.

Truthfully spoken, this connection will change your life, and nothing will ever return to what life was before you awaken to your truth. Most twins get so overwhelmed by their counterpart and the journey that they ask God to send them a high-level soulmate. It's just as loving, caring, and beautiful—and less drama, lol. No, the twin flame journey isn't easy. It's a constant roller coaster of highs, lows, healing, intense emotions, and spiritual attacks, but above all, unconditional love. Love of God, love of the self, and love for your counterpart. From my personal experience, I will tell you, if you are truly on your path, you will see how everything you experienced, including the hurt and the pain and even the attacks, weren't in vain. You will reach the light at the end of the tunnel because God already ordained it so. And that is why I share my truth with you all, but most importantly for the twins in the future who, like me once upon a time ago, were searching for answers and guidance. Always go within, and there is where you will find you and the guidance you seek!

## Chapter 10

# Union

## Song: Let's Get Married
## By: Jagged Edge

The endgame for the twins is union. Some twins come into union, while others don't. That can be for a multitude of reasons. However, one important factor to remember is the union is with the self. Whether you come into union with your destined counterpart or not, the union is manifested within you first. People often spend so much time focusing on the union, they forget to focus on themselves. Union with your counterpart rests on your counterpart's free will. The runner must stop running and start working on healing themselves. The bond between the twins is compelling and life-altering. Whether it brings the best out of you or the worst, it will certainly change your life forever.

True twin flames have adversaries near and far, seen and hidden, all with the same objective: to keep them in separation. This is where the karmics play a prominent role and the very reason why they are sent to the twins in the first place. It's to handle you and distract you from your mission. The reason so many outside influences are invested in keeping these people apart is because they know they are destined to come to together to create something important for the world. The love shared between twins in their truth (all isn't roses) inspires a generation of people to practice love above all. It's easy to hate someone when they are hurting you, but can you still love them despite them showing you who they really are while inflicting so much pain?

Understand unconditional love does not mean tolerating abuse and self-destructive behaviors just because you love someone. Love of the self is first. If you don't love yourself enough to recognize toxic trauma bonds, connections of lust, and unrequited love, you will surely find yourself looped in never-ending cycles of attracting the same type of relationships regardless of who the person is you're in a connection with. All too often we have accepted toxic bonds and a failure to move away from them as some form of loyalty or display of unconditional love on our part. Some of this could be learned behavior, while for others, including myself, it stems from a failure to recognize your own self-worth. But no matter what the excuse is that comes to our mind when we allow this, it's never acceptable. Yes, we deserve more. But in order to receive more, we must first learn to acknowledge and accept that we are more. When you set boundaries and establish higher standards for what you will or will not allow to reside in your life, you truly understand your worth. For those of you guys all the way in the back, in summary, please, just refrain from putting up with toxic bullshit in the name of love . . . It's giving real love an unfair disadvantage to blossom. Thanks kindly.

As much as people love to paint this journey as complete bliss, there is a flip side many twins encounter that several readers and spiritualists don't discuss. There are situations within the twin flame dynamic where one of the counterparts recognizes the other for who they are to them. However, they sabotage the connection out of fear—fear of what they feel toward their counterpart that they never felt toward anyone else, and fear of change. Changing from who they are to who they are supposed to truly be and changing the influences that surround them. Believe it or not, some twins who haven't done the work to heal themselves will often resort to attacking their twin and attempting to destroy their own counterpart. If you're asking yourself how could they do that, the answer is simple: they aren't healed.

They allow outside influences to overpower their own intuition and heart, convincing them to attack their other half, as they witness others in their immediate circle of peers inflict pain on their counterpart out of envy. These group of twins do absolutely nothing to stop the chaos, and this is mainly because these particular twins are dark-natured. They eventually become a karmic masculine or karmic feminine as a consequence of willfully refusing to answer the divine call. They feed their own subconscious with doubt, lies, and negativity about the connection, causing them to run away from the light (their counterpart) straight down the hall to darkness. Many unhealed DMs are notorious for this.

Those twins who are obsessed with their image, people pleasing, and the need for constant attention will abuse their power to manipulate the connection. These are twins who choose (free will) to remain stagnant in toxic lifestyles and mindsets while continuing to engage and interact with toxic people out of a sense of familiarity and comfort. Their refusal to disengage from these toxicities and the paradigm associated with it gives birth to another timeline that, like all causes and effects, comes with consequences. No matter what God has in store for us, ultimately the choice is ours to receive his blessings or to forfeit them. Even though you may be a twin, the choice is always yours to make as to whether you will connect with your counterpart or walk away. Many twins walk away from their counterpart simply because their counterpart is unhealed and refuses to change their behavior.

Truthfully, this connection isn't as common as the masses have been led to believe. There is mostly an imbalance between the twins, where one twin does the work while the other twin runs away from the connection altogether. What you need to understand is neither twin is mandated to be with their counterpart, especially if the other twin is diabolical and refuses to heal. When that occurs, the universe will send the twin who did the work a high-level soulmate, while the twin who refused the call must deal with the consequences of their actions and choices.

Do I want to be in union with my twin? Of course, but not before he is ready, and I wouldn't rush him to be ready if he isn't. I have my journey and he has his, but they intertwine nonetheless. He has lessons to learn, as do I, and I am here to guide him. However, life for me doesn't stop if I am not in physical union with my counterpart. I don't put my life on hold waiting on my masculine, and if you resonate with being a twin flame, neither should you. I sincerely and genuinely love my DM, and no one can ever change that. However, this isn't about people being codependent on each other. This love is solid, and for that reason, the biggest lesson both counterparts learn is the ability to just flow and have no expectations. I didn't say don't have standards and boundaries. Those are values you should never compromise.

This love is ordained by God, if you believe this to be. So, who then can prevent what God has for you? It's never about when you're going to get into union, because you have always been in union with your counterpart. They are the other part of you. The yin and the yang. It's about learning to accept the things you cannot change and still find happiness and love in your heart to know that everything is in accordance with Divine Timing, especially this union. People put people together. But when God puts two people together, let no man put asunder.

The unconditional love felt from the twins to one another gives each the strength and endurance to fight what approaches them another day longer and persevere through the storms. When you get to where I am on the journey, your perception changes and you appreciate why things didn't happen quite the way you once envisioned. A rejection is always for your protection, and it's not always a permanent no, just a simple not now. In other cases, a no is the final decision. No matter how difficult it may be for you to accept this, believe me, it is for your protection because the universe saw things about your twin you didn't see and knows things that they hid from you. The universe might decide that they don't deserve to be with you in the current conditions they've allowed themselves to remain in. Twins, depending on the degree of power they have, can communicate through telepathy, music, and other unconventional methods. This relationship is not about trying to control or manipulate the outcome of the connection. It's about absolute faith in God and his will. It's the epitome of true love. Trust me, any twin flame on the journey will tell you they can write a book about this journey. They are correct, as you can read. I did. These unique connections may seem odd to some, outrageous to others, and downright fictitious for the rest, but as a person who rides the roller coaster of the twin flame journey with others just like me (perhaps you), one thing I think we can collectively agree on is, "You just have to be in it to understand it sometimes."

The reason so many twins get sidetracked on this journey is directly related to expectations. On the journey, expectations are what you should not have, yet you should affirm every day what you know to be truth. It's like this: I affirm my name is Nichole Xenia Clarke. I do not expect everyone to know my name, but as long as I affirm who I am and what my name is and how it is spelled, my name should be addressed as I have affirmed. I can't expect everyone to know my name if I haven't told it to them, nor the spelling. However, once I affirm who I am, there should be no reason for future errors. Expectations equate to disappointments. Expect the unexpected or expect nothing at all, but do not place your hopes, desires, and dreams on expectations, especially when it relates to another individual, because you can only control yourself.

It's with a humbling heart I say thank you to everyone who purchased this book. I do hope you enjoyed my truth, and more importantly, I hope I was able to assist some twins as a guide on their twin flame path should they embark on one. Life won't be the same for us all, but we might all come across the same roads, just on different timelines. If my assistance helps you on your path, then I have done what I was guided to do. For the glory of God.

Namaste . . . As'e

www.ingramcontent.com/pod-product-compliance
Lightning Source LLC
LaVergne TN
LVHW091600060526
838200LV00036B/922